CLARA BARTON

HEALING THE WOUNDS

THE HISTORY OF THE CIVIL WAR

THE HISTORY OF THE CIVIL WAR

CLARA BARTON

HEALING THE WOUNDS

by CATHY EAST DUBOWSKI

INTRODUCTORY ESSAY BY
HENRY STEELE COMMAGER

SILVER BURDETT PRESS

To my mother, Marcella Pugh East, and her mother,
Marcella Hugh Pugh, two very special women

4/92

Series Editorial Supervisor: Richard G. Gallin
Series Editing: Agincourt Press
Series Consultant: Elizabeth Fortson
Cover and Text Design: Circa 86, New York
Series Supervision of Art and Design: Leslie Bauman
Maps: Susan Johnston Carlson

Consultants: Karen Ross, Ph.D. candidate, History of Nursing,
Columbia University; Rudy Johnson, Social Studies Coordinator,
Lansing Public Schools, Lansing, Michigan.

Text Permissions: Mary Norton Papers and Frank Moore Papers,
Manuscript Department, William Perkins Library, Duke University.

Library of Congress Cataloging-in-Publication Data
Dubowski, Cathy East.
    Clara Barton : healing the wounds / by Cathy East Dubowski : with
an introduction by Henry Steele Commager.
       p. cm.—(The History of the Civil War)
    Includes bibliographical references.
    Summary: A biography of the nurse who served on the battlefields
of the Civil War and later founded the American Red Cross.
    1. Barton, Clara, 1821–1912—Juvenile literature. 2. Red Cross-
-United States—Biography—Juvenile literature. 3. Nurses—United
States—Biography—Juvenile literature. 4. United States—History-
-Civil War, 1862–1865—Medical care—Juvenile literature.
[1. Barton, Clara, 1821–1912. 2. Nurses. 3. American National Red
Cross.] I. Title. II. Series.
HV569.B3D83M1990
361.7′634′092—dc20
[B]
[92]   90-8528
  ISBN 0-382-09940-0 (lib bdg.)   ISBN 0-382-24049-9 (pbk.) CIP
                                            AC

TABLE OF CONTENTS

In the Declaration of Independence Thomas Jefferson asserted as a "self-evident truth" that "all men are created equal." This "truth," however, did not encompass women. Nowhere, either in Europe or the new nation of the United States, were women treated equally with men. Their place was thought to be the home—in the kitchen or the nursery. This sphere of influence could occasionally extend to the church or schoolroom. Certainly women did not have equal opportunities in politics. Nor did they achieve even a hope for equality in that realm until 1920, when they won the right to vote.

The situation for women began to change in the 19th century, particularly in education and religion and, more gradually, in nursing. In Europe, almost all teachers were men, but in the United States women slowly replaced men as teachers, and—by the time Clara Barton was born, in 1821—it was taken for granted that the majority of teachers in the schools were women.

Young Clara Barton was one of those women. She was a schoolteacher at 16 and, in one way or another, continued to teach for the rest of her life. By her time, especially in New England, women had begun to take charge of education. Margaret Fuller gave lectures to women on their rights and Elizabeth Peabody introduced the kindergarten from Germany. Young Clara Barton was determined to carve out a career for herself as well.

Eventually Barton grew weary of teaching. For some years she had nursed an invalid brother, and now she wanted to become a nurse. The Civil War gave her a more than ample opportunity. She hurried to Washington, where she helped organize medical support for the army. But Barton was not content with administration. After considerable effort, she obtained permission to nurse wounded soldiers at the actual scene of the fighting. From that point on Barton did much of her nursing on the battlefields. When medicine and supplies ran out, she had recourse to New England towns, many of which responded lavishly to her appeals. In recognition of her services, she was appointed superintendent of nurses.

After Appomattox and the end of the war, Barton went abroad. In Europe, she nursed the wounded on both sides in the Franco-Prussian War, and was honored by kings and emperors for her contributions.

Barton's experience abroad introduced her to the newly-organized International Red Cross, with headquarters in Switzerland. This set the stage for her greatest achievement. Back in her own country she set out to persuade congressmen and senators to commit the United States to join the Red Cross. Inevitably, she was appointed president of the American branch of the organization, and created policy for Red Cross aid in war as well as in domestic disasters. In her old age, she helped establish the American Woman's Suffrage Association, and, not content with that, the Woman's International peace Association.

In all these activities, Barton was a kind of combination of England's Florence Nightingale and America's Julia Ward Howe—a blending of nursing skill and compassion with the desire to uplift and to educate.

CIVIL WAR TIME LINE

May 22
Kansas-Nebraska Act states that in new territories the question of slavery will be decided by the citizens. Many Northerners are outraged because this act could lead to the extension of slavery.

1854	1855	1856	1857

May 21
Lawrence, Kansas is sacked by proslavery Missourians.
May 22
Senator Charles Sumner is caned by Preston Brooks for delivering a speech against slavery.
May 24 – 25
Pottawatomie Creek massacre committed by John Brown and four of his sons.

March 6
The Supreme Court, in the *Dred Scott* ruling, declares that blacks are not U. S. citizens, and therefore cannot bring lawsuits. The ruling divides the country on the question of the legal status of blacks.

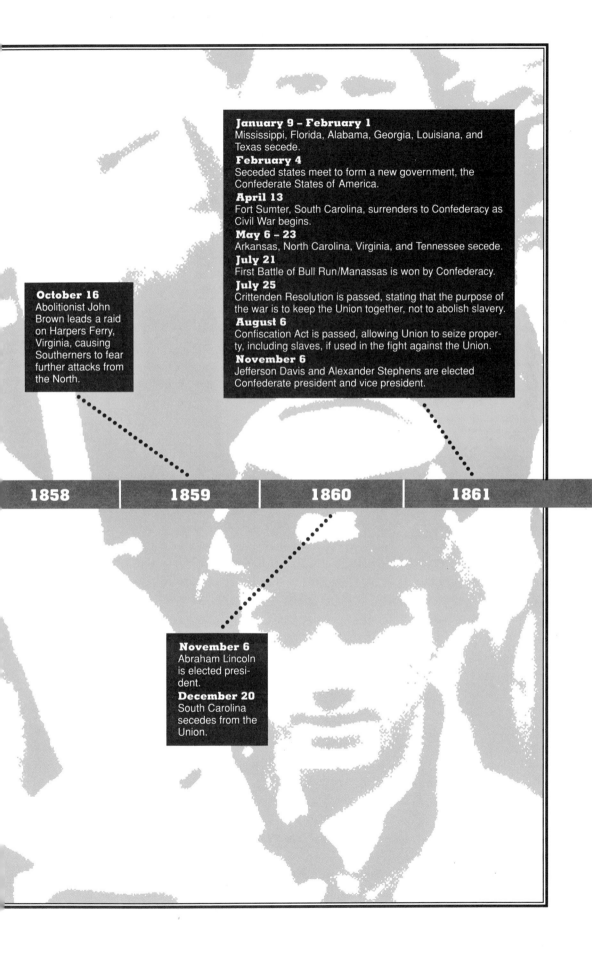

January 9 – February 1
Mississippi, Florida, Alabama, Georgia, Louisiana, and Texas secede.

February 4
Seceded states meet to form a new government, the Confederate States of America.

April 13
Fort Sumter, South Carolina, surrenders to Confederacy as Civil War begins.

May 6 – 23
Arkansas, North Carolina, Virginia, and Tennessee secede.

July 21
First Battle of Bull Run/Manassas is won by Confederacy.

July 25
Crittenden Resolution is passed, stating that the purpose of the war is to keep the Union together, not to abolish slavery.

August 6
Confiscation Act is passed, allowing Union to seize property, including slaves, if used in the fight against the Union.

November 6
Jefferson Davis and Alexander Stephens are elected Confederate president and vice president.

October 16
Abolitionist John Brown leads a raid on Harpers Ferry, Virginia, causing Southerners to fear further attacks from the North.

| 1858 | 1859 | 1860 | 1861 |

November 6
Abraham Lincoln is elected president.

December 20
South Carolina secedes from the Union.

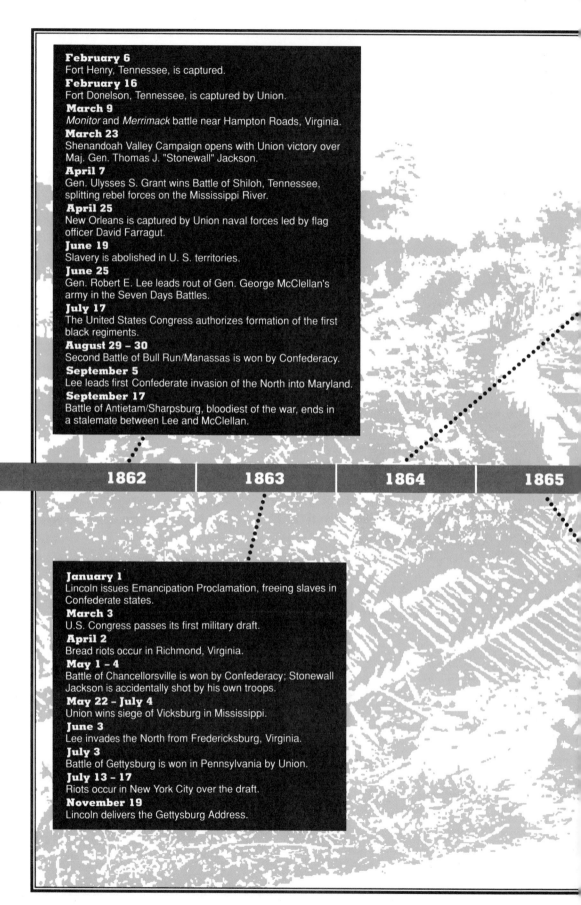

February 6
Fort Henry, Tennessee, is captured.
February 16
Fort Donelson, Tennessee, is captured by Union.
March 9
Monitor and *Merrimack* battle near Hampton Roads, Virginia.
March 23
Shenandoah Valley Campaign opens with Union victory over Maj. Gen. Thomas J. "Stonewall" Jackson.
April 7
Gen. Ulysses S. Grant wins Battle of Shiloh, Tennessee, splitting rebel forces on the Mississippi River.
April 25
New Orleans is captured by Union naval forces led by flag officer David Farragut.
June 19
Slavery is abolished in U. S. territories.
June 25
Gen. Robert E. Lee leads rout of Gen. George McClellan's army in the Seven Days Battles.
July 17
The United States Congress authorizes formation of the first black regiments.
August 29 – 30
Second Battle of Bull Run/Manassas is won by Confederacy.
September 5
Lee leads first Confederate invasion of the North into Maryland.
September 17
Battle of Antietam/Sharpsburg, bloodiest of the war, ends in a stalemate between Lee and McClellan.

1862 | **1863** | **1864** | **1865**

January 1
Lincoln issues Emancipation Proclamation, freeing slaves in Confederate states.
March 3
U.S. Congress passes its first military draft.
April 2
Bread riots occur in Richmond, Virginia.
May 1 – 4
Battle of Chancellorsville is won by Confederacy; Stonewall Jackson is accidentally shot by his own troops.
May 22 – July 4
Union wins siege of Vicksburg in Mississippi.
June 3
Lee invades the North from Fredericksburg, Virginia.
July 3
Battle of Gettysburg is won in Pennsylvania by Union.
July 13 – 17
Riots occur in New York City over the draft.
November 19
Lincoln delivers the Gettysburg Address.

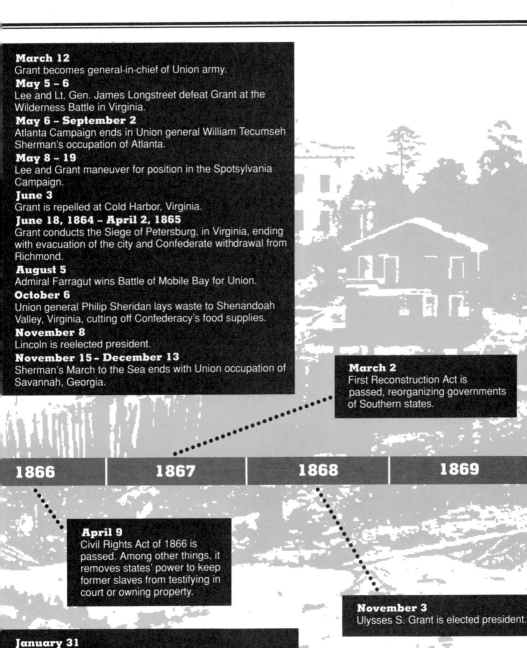

March 12
Grant becomes general-in-chief of Union army.
May 5 – 6
Lee and Lt. Gen. James Longstreet defeat Grant at the Wilderness Battle in Virginia.
May 6 – September 2
Atlanta Campaign ends in Union general William Tecumseh Sherman's occupation of Atlanta.
May 8 – 19
Lee and Grant maneuver for position in the Spotsylvania Campaign.
June 3
Grant is repelled at Cold Harbor, Virginia.
June 18, 1864 – April 2, 1865
Grant conducts the Siege of Petersburg, in Virginia, ending with evacuation of the city and Confederate withdrawal from Richmond.
August 5
Admiral Farragut wins Battle of Mobile Bay for Union.
October 6
Union general Philip Sheridan lays waste to Shenandoah Valley, Virginia, cutting off Confederacy's food supplies.
November 8
Lincoln is reelected president.
November 15 – December 13
Sherman's March to the Sea ends with Union occupation of Savannah, Georgia.

March 2
First Reconstruction Act is passed, reorganizing governments of Southern states.

1866   **1867**   **1868**   **1869**

April 9
Civil Rights Act of 1866 is passed. Among other things, it removes states' power to keep former slaves from testifying in court or owning property.

November 3
Ulysses S. Grant is elected president.

January 31
Thirteenth Amendment, freeing slaves, is passed by Congress and sent to states for ratification.
February 1 – April 26
Sherman invades the Carolinas.
February 6
Lee is appointed general-in-chief of Confederate armies.
March 3
Freedman's Bureau is established to assist former slaves.
April 9
Lee surrenders to Grant at Appomattox Courthouse, Virginia.
April 15
Lincoln dies from assassin's bullet; Andrew Johnson becomes president.
May 26
Remaining Confederate troops surrender.

A HARD CASE

"In the earlier years of my life I remember
nothing but fear."
CLARA BARTON, *THE STORY OF MY CHILDHOOD*

ight-year-old Clara Barton awoke to the sound of a whistle outside. It was still dark. She threw back the covers and ran to open her bedroom window.

It was a clear cold night in North Oxford, Massachusetts. The air smelled crisp and clean. On the ground below, waving wildly at her, were her cousins—Jerry and Otis Learned—and their friend Lovett Stimpson. The blades of the ice skates flung over their shoulders flashed like knives in the moonlight. They had an extra pair, they whispered up at her. Come on, they said. They would teach her how to skate.

Clara's father, Stephen Barton, had only recently moved his family to the Learned farm. His favorite nephew, Jeremiah Learned, had died after a long illness. That left Jeremiah's wife and four children with a huge run-down farm that was deeply in debt. Clara's father and another relative bought the farm in 1830, but he let the Learned family stay on. Clara's father had also taken charge of raising Lovett Stimpson, the son of a friend.

What a change it was for Clara! In her old home, she had no playmates at all. She had always been terribly shy. Here everything was so different. "I now found myself one of a very lively body of six—three boys and three girls nearer of an age than would have been probable in the same family," Clara wrote years later in her autobiography, *The Story of My Childhood*. These daring cousins roamed the hillsides with a spirit and freedom that Clara had never known. She adored Jerry and Otis. She tried hard to keep up with them, to earn their praise. When they saw that she could run and ride horses "like a boy," they became fast friends.

They dared one another to cross the French River on a narrow teetering pole. They explored the farm's barns, brooks, and caves. At the sawmill, they played with little care for the danger. "Hurt? Never one of us. Killed? We knew not such a thing could be."

Clara had been so timid for so long. Now this wild, free play with her cousins was like a key—it unlocked a hunger in her for adventure. In the early 19th century, girls were not taught to be athletic. Certainly they did not compete with boys. Perhaps that was part of the excitement. To hold her own with the boys gave Clara a new sense of self-worth. Their praise made her feel special.

Clara's parents were eager for her to get over her shyness. But now they worried that she was becoming a tomboy. Among other things, her father had forbidden her to learn to skate.

"Skating had not then become customary, in fact, not even allowable for girls," remembered Clara. Neither she nor the boys could understand why.

Now Clara looked out her bedroom window as Jerry, Otis, and Lovett stamped their feet in the cold.

"Come on," they said eagerly.

Clara hesitated. What would she do? It was early Sunday morning. It would be hours before the others would be awake. Clara could slip out and be back before anyone knew she was gone. Of course, her parents would not like it. It was breaking the Sabbath....

"Hurry!" cried the boys.

Clara could not say no. "The ice was so smooth and 'glare,'" she remembered. "The stars were bright, the temptation was too great. I was in my dress in a moment and out."

Giggling and shushing one another, the four friends ran through the darkness for the ice. Quickly they fastened their skates. One of the boys tied his wool scarf around Clara's waist so he could pull her. The other two boys stood on either side of her to keep her steady. Then off they glided into the moonlight.

More and more swiftly the little skating party flew across the ice. Suddenly they came to a spot where the ice was rough and cracked. Clara fell and tumbled across the jagged ice, badly cutting her knees. "There was more blood flowing than any of us had ever seen," she remembered.

Clara and the boys were terrified. Now they would surely get caught. Clara's cut knees were quickly bound up with the wool scarves. Then her friends helped her hobble home. Her long petticoats and skirt would hide her bandaged knees. Maybe no one would find out.

Bravely Clara kept her pain a secret. By the next day, however, her knees were much worse. Soon her wounds—and her deeds—

were discovered. The blood had dried, and the stiff scarves had to be soaked off. A doctor was called. One knee was quite serious, he said. He put her to bed with her bad leg propped up on a chair. She stayed there for three weeks.

Clara's parents did not punish her, but for Clara their kindness was even worse. So she punished herself, brooding for hours over how badly she had behaved.

Sarah Barton tried to tell her daughter that what she had done was not so bad. In fact, she herself had once ridden an unbroken horse against her father's wishes—and had been thrown. Somehow that did not make Clara feel any better.

"When I saw how genuinely they all pitied, and how tenderly they nursed me, in spite of my disobedience and . . . all the trouble I had caused, my mental suffering far exceeded my physical," Clara remembered. "I despised myself, and failed to sleep or eat."

When Clara was almost well, she heard the doctor tell her father, "That was a hard case, Captain, but she stood it like a soldier."

Clarissa Harlow Barton was born on Christmas Day, 1821, in a home her father had built with his own hands in North Oxford, Massachusetts. She was named for an aunt, who had been named for Clarissa Harlowe, the heroine in a popular novel. No one ever called her that, though. She was always just Clara.

The Barton family greeted this Christmas baby as an interesting little treasure—for all her brothers and sisters were much older than she. The youngest one, Sally, was almost 11 by the time Clara was born. David was 13, Stephen was 15, and Dorothea, known as Dolly, was 17. Her father, Stephen Barton, was well into his forties by then, and her mother, Sarah Stone Barton, was 34. For Clara, it was like being born into a family of grown-ups.

To this grown-up family, Clara was like a Christmas present. In many ways she was always their toy—something to play with, to brag about, to protect, to spoil.

The Barton household was a lively, noisy place to grow up, for all the Bartons had strong wills and spirited tempers. At times, Clara was the center of attention. At other times, she was forgotten as adult business took center stage. In many ways she was always separate and alone. She spent her childhood trying to "catch up"— and to measure up—to her adored brothers and sisters.

"I had no playmates, but in effect six fathers and mothers," she later wrote. "They were a family of schoolteachers. All took charge of me, all educated me, each according to personal taste."

The Bartons were an old New England family—hardworking, careful with their money, independent, and self-sufficient—with a colorful history. Bartons were among the first American colonists. Samuel Barton, the first to come to North Oxford, defended a woman accused of being a witch at the Salem witch trials in Massachusetts. Clara's grandfather, Dr. Stephen Barton, fought in the American Revolution.

His son, also named Stephen, was Clara's father. He was a moral man, who believed in the New England idea of hard work. Though the Barton family was prosperous, he worked the family farm and mill with his own hands, and built much of the household's furniture. Yet he was a witty man who had many modern ideas. He believed in reading and education. He was active in town government and spent his own money to help the poor. The Barton home was always open to visitors who wanted to discuss new ideas.

As a young man, Stephen Barton had served as a soldier in the Northwest Territory under General "Mad Anthony" Wayne. There he fought in what were known as Indian wars, a long series of struggles between white settlers and Native American Indians over land. One of Clara's earliest pleasures was to play soldier and listen to stories of her father's adventures.

"His soldier habits and tastes never left him," Clara said. "And very naturally my father became my instructor in military and political lore. I listened breathlessly to his war stories. Illustrations were called for, and we made battles and fought them."

Neither Clara nor her father could imagine that one day she would find herself on a battlefield, and that these playful "lessons" would serve her well. "When later, I, like all the rest of our country's people, was suddenly thrust into the mysteries of war, and had to find and take my place and part in it, I found myself far less a stranger to the conditions than most women, or even ordinary men for that matter."

Captain Barton had married Sarah Stone when he was 30 and she was only 17. A strong-minded woman with a fiery temper, Sarah was quick to swear and was known for being thrifty and eccentric. She "always did two days' work in one, never slept after 3 o'clock, both *nervy* and *nervous,*" wrote Clara.

With so many others in the household to care for and teach the baby daughter, her mother, in Clara's words, "attempted very little." But Clara could not help but learn from her colorful mother that women could think for themselves and have their own ideas. Clara's mother signed antislavery petitions in the early days of the abolitionist movement, which was made up of people who wanted to abolish, or end, slavery. The abolitionists believed that all slaves should be freed at once, without compensating the slave owners in any way for their financial loss. Her mother was also an outspoken feminist, someone who believed that women should have the same rights and freedoms as men.

By age three, Clara could read and spell. Before she was four, the family sent her off through the New England snowdrifts on the shoulders of her brother Stephen to "regular school." Most schools of the day were not divided into grades. Students of all ages were often crowded together in one-room schools. In this school, Clara was clearly the baby.

Clara was placed in a crowded room clutching her spelling book and slate. Soon the teacher, Colonel Richard Stone, called the youngest to the front. He pointed out the letters of the alphabet. Clara knew them all. When he asked Clara to read some simple words like *dog* and *cat,* she politely told him she did "not spell there."

"Where do you spell?" asked Stone.

"I spell in 'Artichoke,'" she said. She pointed in her spelling book to the top word in a column of hard three-syllable words. It was clear to Stone that Clara would be one of his best pupils.

Schools at that time taught reading, writing, and arithmetic—
and little else. Stone, however, was well-known throughout New
England for offering his students more. Sometime during the
school year, Clara was given a copy of *Menseur's Geography.* Unlike
many textbooks of the day, this one had been written just for
children. Clara "became so interested that I could not sleep, and was
not willing that others should. [I woke] my poor drowsy sister in
the cold winter mornings to sit up in my bed and by the light of a
tallow candle, help me to find mountains, rivers, counties, oceans,
lakes, islands, isthmuses, channels, cities, towns and capitals."

Meanwhile, her brothers and sisters continued to teach her. "My
elder brother, Stephen, was a noted mathematician," remembered
Clara. "He inducted me into the mystery of figures."

Brother David was a daredevil who loved horses. "One could
almost add that he was fond of nothing else," said Clara. When she
was five, David would throw her upon a horse with only bridle
and bit and call out, "Cling fast to the mane!" Then they would
gallop wildly across the fields.

"They were merry rides we took," Clara remembered. "To this
day my seat on a saddle or on the back of a horse is as secure and
tireless as in a rocking chair, and far more pleasurable. Sometimes,
in later years, when I found myself suddenly on a strange horse in a
trooper's saddle, flying for life or liberty...I blessed the baby
lessons of the wild gallops among the beautiful colts."   -

David also taught her many things usually reserved for boys. He
was a strict teacher, too. She must throw a ball "like a boy." She
must hit a nail straight on the head and not split the board. She
must tie a square knot that would hold.

"I recall no season of dolls," wrote Clara, "and believe they were
never included in my [education]."

Even the family dog helped look after Clara. Button was a
chipper white dog with sparkling black eyes. He followed her
everywhere and even slept at the foot of her bed.

Clara could ride as well, and run as fast, as any boy. She could do
figures, play soldiers, and write poetry. Still she often felt hope-

lessly inferior to the other members of her family. Often, when she tried to add to the grown-up conversation, the family would laugh in amusement. That only made her more self-conscious about everything she said. So did the constant teasing she received as the baby of the family.

Once she was given a cake, which she wanted to share with everyone. The family gathered around—including Button—and Clara counted how many pieces were needed. Carefully she cut the cake and handed out the pieces. The last one went to Button, who quickly finished his share.

Only then did Clara look at her empty hands. She had forgotten to add herself to the count! The whole family laughed at the joke Clara had played on herself. Clara said nothing. She was too embarrassed. Her brothers and sisters tried to give her their piece, but Clara's mother said no. "I must not be taught to think I could give a thing and still possess it," Clara wrote. "A gift must be outright." Such experiences were, in Clara's words, an "opportunity for an amusing bit of sport for the family at my expense." The teasing was probably all in fun, but Clara took it all to heart.

In 1828, when Clara was six, her sister Dolly had a nervous breakdown. In the early 19th century, people were ashamed of mental illness. They did not talk about it, and few people believed it could be treated or cured. Dolly became violent. Eventually the Bartons had to lock her in a room with bars on the window. It was hard for Clara to see her sister in such a state. In her autobiography, she described Dolly only as "an invalid."

Clara's sister Sally, who also taught school, now paid more attention to her younger sister and led her into a world of literature and poetry. Yet Clara was growing more and more timid. She hid from strangers. She was afraid to speak up when she wanted or needed something. Her family was very worried about her. The shyer she got, the more they discussed her problem—often right in front of her as if she were not there. Finally they decided they would never be able to "cure" her shyness at home. It was not unusual for young girls to go away to boarding school. Perhaps that was just what Clara needed.

When she was eight, the Bartons "decided to throw me among strangers," as Clara put it. Maybe then, away from her protective family, she would grow independent and sure of herself.

But the experience had the opposite effect.

Clara was sent to a new boarding school run by Colonel Richard Stone, who had been her very first teacher. Again she was the youngest, but here there were 150 students. She was short, plump, and plain. She talked with a childish lisp, which embarrassed her when she had to speak in front of the older students. More than once she fled the classroom in tears. Her studies gave her no trouble, but she wrote, "I was in constant dread of doing something wrong."

The more she withdrew, the more she drew unwanted attention. "I grew very tired, felt hungry all the time, but dared not eat, grew thin and pale." Finally Colonel Stone, Clara's father, and the family doctor decided she should come home.

Soon afterwards, the family moved to the Learned farm. Clara's father sold the family's two hill farms to Clara's brothers. Both grown now, Stephen and David had gone into business together. Her unmarried sisters lived with the brothers.

The new home was a run-down early 18th-century farmhouse. Clara was fascinated by the many workmen who came to do the repairs. Clara was especially captivated by a painter named Sylvanus Harris. It was a time when painters still made many of their own materials, from grinding their own paint and mixing colors to making their own putty.

One day Clara gathered her courage and asked him, "Will you teach me to paint, sir?"

"With pleasure," said Mr. Harris, "if mama is willing."

Her mother gave her permission, and Clara became a devoted, hardworking helper. She learned to mix paints, boil oil, and trim and hang wallpaper, and she even varnished the kitchen chairs. When the work was finished, Clara was heartbroken. Later, alone in her room, she found a box on her candle stand. In it was a pretty locket, which was engraved: "To a faithful worker." It was Clara's first "medal" for a job well done, but it would not be her last.

Clara's life during these years appears to have been a seesaw of joys and disappointments. She seemed happy only when she was busy—a feeling that would often drive her in her adult life. She found freedom and fulfillment in the athletic world of her cousins and in her academic successes. But she felt guilty when she failed to be what society—and her parents—thought a "proper" little girl should be.

After her skating accident, her parents began to push her into friendships with girls, such as her cousin Elvira Stone and a neighbor, Nancy Fitts. There were tea parties and playhouses. Her mother taught her to cook and sew. But Clara found a girl's world filled with no's, don't, and can'ts. When a family friend opened a dancing school, Clara was not allowed to attend. The family decided that it was not proper for a girl her age to take lessons at a hotel.

Often Clara found joy in caring for the farm's many animals. A visitor gave her 30 duck eggs, which she managed to hatch with the help of some hens. In two or three years, her flock was so large it attracted migrating wild ducks. She often adopted the farm's livestock as pets.

One day as she went to look for her favorite cows, she came upon several field hands. To her horror, she saw them slaughter a large red ox with an ax. Clara fainted on the spot.

When she came to in bed, her family asked her why she had fallen. "Someone struck me," she said, and she would not believe otherwise. "Happy ignorance!" she later wrote. "I had not then learned the mystery of nerves."

After that, Clara recalled, "I lost all desire for meat, if I had ever had it—and all through life to the present, have only eaten it when I must for the sake of appearance.... The bountiful ground has always yielded enough for all my needs and wants."

By the time Clara was 11, her grown brothers were busy with a new mill business. Sally was married. Mrs. Learned had moved away to open a boardinghouse, taking Clara's cousins with her. Once again, Clara felt very much alone.

Then suddenly "an accidental turn in my wheel of fortune changed my entire course..." Clara wrote in her autobiography, "and how much bearing, if any, it may have had on the future, I have never been able to determine."

Clara's brother David was helping to build a new barn when he fell from the roof and was badly hurt. "I was distressed beyond measure at his condition," Clara recalled. "From the first days and nights of illness, I remained near his side....I learned to take all directions for his medicines from his physician...and to administer them like a genuine nurse."

For his headaches and fever, the family doctor prescribed *leeching*. This was a common cure-all used to treat everything from headaches to broken bones. Slimy black leeches were applied to the patient's main veins to suck out the "bad blood." When the leeches were full, they fell off and were kept in jars for later use.

At first, Clara was terrified by the leeches. But her love for David changed that. "My little hands became schooled to the handling of the great, loathsome crawling leeches which were at first so many snakes to me, and no fingers could so painlessly dress the angry blisters; and thus it came about, that I was the accepted and acknowledged nurse of a man almost too ill to recover.

Leeching, in fact, was bad medicine. It weakened patients as it robbed them of much-needed blood. Instead of getting better, David grew worse. Clara insisted on staying with him night and day. Soon David wanted no one but his little sister by his side. For two years she devoted herself to him, attending to his every need. It was a dark, sad time. Yet something positive was happening in Clara's life. To be needed so badly filled a strong need in Clara herself. For the rest of her life, she was never so happy as when devoting herself to an urgent need that she felt only she could meet.

"I realize now how carefully and [nervously] the whole family watched the little nurse," wrote Clara, "but I had no idea of it then. I thought my position the most natural thing in the world; I almost forgot that there was an outside to the house."

Doctors from miles around discussed David's case. At last the leeches were replaced with something called a "steam cure" and good food. Only then did David slowly regain his strength.

Clara was thrilled at her brother's recovery, but she also felt a deep sense of loss at no longer being needed. "I was again free; my occupation gone. Life seemed very strange and idle to me.... in the two years I had not grown an inch, had been to school one-half day, and had gained one pound in weight."

Caring for her brother had given Clara a sense of purpose. But her two-year separation from the rest of the world had made her even more timid around people outside the family. Once again, she felt unimportant and useless.

To fill her need, she followed her father's example and devoted herself to charity work. She tutored poor children. She nursed several families during a smallpox epidemic until she herself became ill with the disease.

Highlights in the Life of Clara Barton

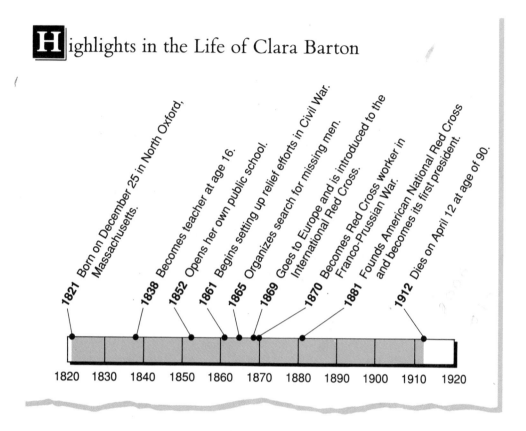

1821 Born on December 25 in North Oxford, Massachusetts.

1838 Becomes teacher at age 16.

1852 Opens her own public school.

1861 Begins setting up relief efforts in Civil War.

1865 Organizes search for missing men.

1869 Goes to Europe and is introduced to the International Red Cross.

1870 Becomes Red Cross worker in Franco-Prussian War.

1881 Founds American National Red Cross and becomes its first president.

1912 Dies on April 12 at age of 90.

1820 1830 1840 1850 1860 1870 1880 1890 1900 1910 1920

When she was older, her brothers opened up the Satinet Mill of North Oxford, which made a fine-quality satinlike cloth. The United States was awakening to new ways of making goods with powerful machines—changes brought about by the invention of the steam engine. The Bartons embraced these new ideas. They, with many others, helped make New England the birthplace of the American industrial revolution.

Until that time, about the only acceptable occupation for young unmarried women was teaching. The cloth mills, however, created a new demand for skilled hands, and women began to fill the new factories. Touring the mill, Clara was impressed by the skill of the young women who worked as weavers. "I astonished the family by announcing my desire to go into the mill. I wanted to weave cloth."

At first her family only laughed at her. Then they said she was too small, and this work was not proper. But her brother Stephen stood up for her and arranged to let her try.

The next day, Clara went to work and threw herself into her task. Soon her work was judged to be as fine as any in the mill.

A few Sundays later, when the mill sat empty, a fire burned the factory to the ground. "The strong energetic brothers knew the rebuilding would begin at once, but I mourned without hope," wrote Clara. Even then, Clara's family could not resist a bit of fun. They joked that Clara had worked so fast, the friction had set the mill on fire. "That joke on me lasted many years," wrote Clara.

One day 16-year-old Clara, sick with the mumps, was lying on the sofa in the sitting room. To her dismay, she heard her mother in the next room pouring out her worries about her shy, "difficult" daughter to a visitor, L. W. Fowler. Fowler was a popular lecturer on *phrenology,* a forerunner to psychology. It was based on the idea that different behaviors were controlled by different parts of the brain. Personality traits, it said, could be determined by "reading" the bumps on the skull. One of its goals was to help find out what a person was best suited for.

Fowler's "reading" of Clara's personality was that she suffered much more from her shyness and sensitivity than her friends and family did. These traits, he said, "may be apparently outgrown, but the sensitive nature will always remain. She will never assert herself for herself—she will suffer wrong first—but for others she will be perfectly fearless."

"What shall I do?" asked Clara's mother.

"Throw responsibility on her," Fowler replied. "She has all the qualities of a teacher. As soon as her age will permit, give her a school to teach."

Listening in the next room, Clara was shocked. She could not imagine that she would ever be able to stand in front of a classroom of strangers and speak, much less teach.

But a year later she would be doing just that.

THE SHY STUDENT BECOMES A TEACHER

"Child that I was, I did not know that the surest
test of discipline is its absence."

CLARA BARTON, *THE STORY OF MY CHILDHOOD*

On a beautiful morning in May 1838, Clara Barton hurried down the road to a one-room schoolhouse in North Oxford. It was her first day as teacher. Seventeen and a half years old but only five feet tall, she looked like a child herself. She had spent days lengthening skirts and learning to put up her hair so she would look taller and older.

A person did not need a college degree to become a teacher then. Most women did not even go to college. Barton only had to pass a teacher's examination. A committee rated her "excellent."

Inside the school, she faced 40 children, ages 4 to 13. Four tough-looking boys, as tall as Barton and almost as old, stared at her mischievously. She had heard about them. Last term, they had locked the teacher out and taken over the school.

Barton was too terrified even to say good morning. Instead she picked up her Bible and told her students to take turns reading.

At one passage, she asked her students what they thought Jesus meant when he said that they must love their enemies. At first no one answered. Then a tiny girl said, "I think He meant that you

must be good to everybody, and mustn't quarrel or make nobody feel bad, and I'm going to try."

Barton's praise stopped the smirks of the four older boys. They caused no trouble that day, and Barton was relieved—but still wary.

A day or two later, during recess, she decided she did not like the older boys' rough, unfair play. She decided they "needed teaching, even to play well." So Barton, who had been well taught by her brothers and cousins, joined in the boys' game.

"My four lads soon perceived that I was no stranger to their sports or their tricks...that they were not the first boys I had seen." When they found that she could run and throw a ball as well as they could, she earned their admiration and respect.

The rest of the spring term went beautifully. Barton's own love of learning inspired her students. Perhaps her painful memories of being a shy student made her an especially loving teacher.

Spankings and beatings were common in schools at the time, but they were teaching tools Barton never used. So she was surprised when the town gave her school top honors for discipline. She insisted that "there had been no discipline, that not one scholar had ever been disciplined. Child that I was, I did not know that the surest test of discipline is its absence."

Word quickly spread about Barton's school. She was overwhelmed with offers to teach in Oxford and other nearby towns. Saying no was out of the question. Her family was much too happy with her success to let her give up such an acceptable occupation.

For the next 10 years, Barton taught at many schools. Her students gave her the approval she had always longed for. Her work gave her a sense of identity and seemed to ease her shyness. Most of all, she enjoyed "straightening out" a problem school. L. W. Fowler's predictions for her seemed to have been correct.

The busier Barton became, the more her shyness faded. She had always felt homely, but many young men found her attractive. She often wore red, which set off her shiny dark hair and dark brown eyes. She loved to laugh and became quite a wit. Perhaps she liked the power of creating the laughter rather than being the object of the joke, as she often felt had happened when she was a child.

It was an age when all young girls were expected to marry. They were not thought to be equal to men. They could not vote. They were barred from most careers. Education was not thought to be very important for a woman, whose future held only marriage and children.

But Barton could ride a horse as well as any man and had studied philosophy and other "male" subjects. She grew up assuming she was equal to men, and she disliked men who did not respect women or who treated them like children. The very things that made Barton special made it hard for her to find her match in a man. She had special friendships with men, but none led to marriage.

Barton stayed busy, but not just with teaching and social activities. She often kept the books for her brothers' mill. She helped raise money for a new Universalist church, then scraped up paint and nailed down carpet as it was built.

By the time Barton was 29, however, she grew more and more restless. She had no prospects for marriage. Even worse, she was running out of challenges in North Oxford. She began to have those old thoughts of feeling useless. She began to feel sorry for herself. She had loved teaching. But as she watched her students grow up and get on with their own lives, she began to question her own. "I decided that I must withdraw and find a school, the object of which should be to teach *me* something."

The year 1850 offered few choices to women who wanted higher education. After much thought, Barton chose the Clinton Liberal Institute, in Clinton, New York. It was 200 miles away—a full three days' journey from Oxford.

Barton kept her plans to herself until the last minute. When she told her family, they were shocked. In an age without cars and planes, a 200-mile trip was a major event. Her mother was ill, too. But the decision had been made.

In December 1850, Barton bundled herself and her belongings into her brother Stephen's sleigh. With a shake of the reins, they dashed off through the snow for the train station.

Clara Barton was leaving home.

The Clinton Liberal Institute was run by the Universalist Church. It had a daring policy of encouraging young women to take courses in mathematics and science—subjects usually reserved for males. Barton attacked her studies with the same devotion that she had used to raise ducks or nurse her brother David.

Still, it was not an easy year. Barton had to learn to live independently, without her strong family to look after her. She paid her own way—the large sum of $35 a term for tuition, room and board. Her small savings from teaching left no money for extras. She was a good 10 years older than most of the other students, although she did not look it. She wanted to fit in, so she kept her age a secret and did not talk about her years of teaching. She spent most of her time studying or writing letters.

However, she did become good friends with a 16-year-old girl named Mary Norton. Mary's brother, Charles, also attended the

Institute, and he developed quite a crush on Barton. The Nortons helped draw her away from too many long hours of studying.

In May of 1851, Barton received shocking news. Her brother Stephen had been arrested for robbing a bank in New York. He was not convicted, but the suspicions remained.

Then, in July, Stephen wrote that their mother had died. By the time Barton got his letter, her mother had already been buried. Barton told no one at school, and suffered through her grief alone, 200 miles from home.

When the school year was over, Barton had satisfied her desire for more education. Back home at North Oxford, however, too many things had changed. Her mother was gone, and her father was living with her brother David. Her schools were doing fine. Barton did not feel needed. More than ever, she felt unsure now of what she wanted to do with her life. She wanted to leave, but she had no idea where to go or what she would do to earn her living.

That fall, Mary and Charles Norton gave her her chance. Mary wrote and begged her to come for a visit in Hightstown, New Jersey. Happily, Barton said yes. In mid-October she left home, not knowing what might happen, but eager for change.

The Norton family drew Barton into a whirl of social activity. Many evenings, the Nortons' home was filled with piano music and the laughter of parlor games.

At first Barton had a wonderful time, but she was never happy for long without work. The Nortons noticed a restlessness in her, too. Mr. Norton was hesitant when he told her about an opening for a teacher. He did not know of Barton's years of teaching. This job was in nearby Cedarville, at a school known for its rough boys. Might she be interested? Mr. Norton asked. She was welcome to continue living in the Norton home if she liked. Barton said she would give it a try. Secretly she smiled. She knew what to do.

The first day of school arrived. Barton stood in front of the classroom and looked around at the faces of her new students. Then she called on the biggest, toughest-looking boy in the room. She told him to take the last teacher's switches into the yard—and break them into tiny pieces! The boy was amazed. Then Barton explained that she would never need those switches. She knew she could count on him to help set an example for good behavior. From that moment on the children loved her.

One thing troubled Barton, though. Unlike the free schools she had known in Massachusetts, these schools were "subscription schools." The children had to pay to come and learn. Free public schools were a new idea, and there were none at all in New Jersey. Many people saw free schools as charity rather than a right. Barton's salary came from billing the students at the end of each term. She hated it so much that she asked Mary or Charles to do it for her.

By the end of the school year, however, Barton was feeling restless again. She loved the Nortons, but there was never any privacy. The house was always filled with people, and her friends always insisted that she join in everything they did. Something else was bothering her, too. During the year, Barton had won the attentions of several young men, including Charles. She enjoyed their friendship but took none of them seriously. Her heart belonged to a farmer named Joshua Ely, who lived near Philadelphia.

No one quite knows how she came to know him, but she and "JLE," as she called him in her diary, wrote often. Suddenly, in early spring, his letters stopped coming. Barton worried that he might be sick or hurt. At last she went to see him to find out what was wrong. She never told anyone what happened on that visit, and she stopped writing in her diary for a month. It was clear that somehow the romance had ended.

As the days went by, Barton grew more and more depressed. She saw herself turning into what people cruelly called a "spinster"—an old unmarried woman in a society that valued women only for their homes and children. She saw no career choices open to her that would ever earn more than just enough money to get by. As always, she kept all these feelings to herself. One day she simply announced to the Nortons that she was making the 10-mile trip to nearby Bordentown, New Jersey. Her friends took her to the train station, chatting gaily about all the things they would do when she returned.

Barton climbed on the train and waved good-bye—knowing she would never come back.

Barton had no job and no plans. As she walked the streets of Bordentown, she was amazed at the number of boys she saw who were not in school. There were no free schools here, either. Barton talked with them and asked why they were not in school.

"Lady, there is no school for us," one poorly dressed 14-year-old told her. "We would be glad to go if there was one."

Here was a need—a challenge. Barton flew into action. She visited Peter Suydam, editor of the *Bordentown Register* and chairman of the school committee. She told him that she wanted to open a free public school in Bordentown—and teach there herself.

Suydam did not think it was a good idea. These were rough boys, more suited for jail than school. Even a *man* would have trouble handling them. The state had had laws since 1817 allowing free public schools, but the people were still cold to the idea. Parents would be embarrassed to send their children to a "pauper's school." The teachers of paid schools—many of whom were important society women—would be against her.

But Barton had her own list of all the *good* reasons to open her school. For 10 years she had taught in some of New England's toughest schools. She had met the boys on the streets here and did not fear them. She did not care a whit what "society" people thought. To top it off, she said she would work without pay. If the committee would support her and give her a building, she would take care of the rest.

Suydam was impressed. He talked to the school committee that evening. The next day, Clara Barton had her school.

She started out with an old closed-down school building. The school committee saw that the building was cleaned and that new benches were built. Barton ordered maps and even a blackboard.

At last the school was ready. The school committee put up posters and placed ads in the newspaper. Barton could hardly wait. But when the first day came, only six boys showed up. Barton taught as if she had a whole roomful of children—and the next day twenty children came.

Each day her class grew. Most of the children had had little education, and they were hungry to learn. Barton did not stop with reading, writing, and arithmetic. She led them into all kinds of new subjects. She even shared books such as *Uncle Tom's Cabin* with them. Written by Harriet Beecher Stowe, it was the story of a good slave who was beaten to death by his cruel master. It was a controversial book; slavery was one of many issues that were beginning to divide the country. It deeply touched Barton's sense of human rights.

Soon after school started, Barton wrote to Mary Norton: "I suppose you have read *Uncle Tom's Cabin*—isn't it excellent.... My school boys, poor fellows, are reading and crying over it and wishing all sorts of good luck to Uncle Tom."

Though Barton's school started with just boys, she found room for the girls, too. The school grew so quickly that Fanny Childs, a friend of Barton's from North Oxford, was hired to teach the younger children. Once Mr. Suydam had feared the townspeople would fight Barton's ideas. Now they were so proud, they raised the teachers' salaries to a high $250 a year.

Free public schools were a wonderful success in Bordentown, thanks to Barton. She had become a local hero and was busier and happier than she had ever been. The school that had started with six boys now had more than 200 students. Four hundred more wanted to come. The townspeople voted $4,000 for a new school with rooms for all 600 children. When finished, it would be two stories tall, hold the latest maps and school equipment, and have enough room and teachers to allow children to be taught in grades. It was a sweet triumph for Barton.

But it was soon to be stolen from her—because she was a woman.

When Schoolhouse Number 1 opened in the fall of 1853, Barton was shocked to learn that she would not be the principal of the school she had founded. No one questioned Barton's skills as a teacher. But in the 1850s, few women held top positions of authority. Many people thought the Bordentown public school had become much too large and important for a woman to run. A man

UNCLE TOM'S CABIN;

OR,

LIFE AMONG THE LOWLY.

BY

HARRIET BEECHER STOWE.

VOL. I.

BOSTON:
JOHN P. JEWETT & COMPANY.
CLEVELAND, OHIO:
JEWETT, PROCTOR & WORTHINGTON.
1852.

When *Uncle Tom's Cabin* was published in 1852, it brought to light many of the evils of slavery.

named J. Kirby Burnham was brought in—at more than twice her salary—to take over the school. Barton was made a "female assistant."

Barton was crushed. She did not believe in Burnham's strict rules for the children. She felt he was unkind to her and found fault with all her work. Quarrels broke out among the teachers. Fanny Childs and one or two other teachers took Barton's side. Others sided with Burnham. Several religious groups began to complain that the school committee should give their schools money, too. Many of the paying schools closed down as their students changed to the free school, and their teachers were angry. The quarrels divided the townspeople.

Barton's joy in her new school was ruined. She became nervous and depressed. Perhaps in her unhappiness, she stopped eating, the way she had as a child. Soon her health began to fail. She grew pale and weak. Finally she completely lost her voice. It was a pattern that would repeat itself throughout her life, whenever she suffered from stress or disappointment.

At last Barton could no longer stand the strain. She resigned.

It was a bitter time for Barton. She was 32. She did not know what she wanted to do, but she knew she did not want to move back home. Finally she decided to go to Washington, D.C., to recover.

After nearly 15 years of successful teaching, she had no way of knowing she was leaving the classroom forever.

3

WASHINGTON AND WAR

"Men talk flippantly of dissolving the Union.
This may happen, but in my humble opinion
never till our very horses gallop in human
blood."

CLARA BARTON, *In a letter
to her brother Stephen*

ashington, D.C., in 1854 was a rowdy half-built town
with 50,000 people. The unpaved streets were lined with
boardinghouses. The water and sewage systems were
crude. People came and went with the changes of the political
calender.

For Barton, it was a wonderful place to slow down and get well.
She spent hours reading in the Library of Congress. She listened to
the long debates in the Senate and House of Representatives, and
she soon learned a lot about politics and current events. Her voice
came back, and her health improved. But Barton never cared much
for long vacations. Soon she looked around for something useful
that she could do.

Barton found a good friend in Alexander DeWitt, a congressman from her home district. He introduced her to Charles Mason,
commissioner of the U.S. Patent Office. Mason gave her a job as a
temporary clerk in the Patent Office.

In 1854, few women worked for the federal government. Many
politicians thought hiring women took good jobs away from men.
Many thought it improper for women to mix with men in the

same office. Not only was Barton a woman, she was smart and ambitious. Many of her male co-workers resented her—especially when they learned she was being paid $1,400 a year. That was the same pay a male clerk got. Some of the men blew cigar smoke in her face and spread gossip about her, but Barton paid little attention. She was too happy with her new job.

The Patent Office, set up in 1836, was one of the most interesting offices in Washington. It granted *patents*—which gave a person the sole right to make and sell his or her invention. This legally prevented others from stealing the idea. In the early years, the office was active in scientific research and paid for scientific trips. One new wing was like a museum, filled with historical and scientific treasures from around the world.

Barton worked hard as a clerk. There were no computers, photocopying machines, or typewriters, so clerks spent hours writing page after page of legal documents by hand. Still, Barton wrote in her letters to friends and family that her job was delightful.

Outside of work, Clara was being drawn into Washington's social whirl. She soon had a large circle of friends, many of them important people in the government. For the first time in her life, she was able to save a little money, which added to her sense of independence.

But then as now, the security of many government jobs depended upon the winds of politics—and by the 1850s, a serious storm was brewing.

During the American Revolution, the 13 original colonies had fought a common enemy. Together they had forged a new nation and created a new form of government free from the whims of a king or queen. Though each state kept its own identity, all were united in a common cause. As the years passed, however, the states in the North and the states in the South had grown apart.

In the middle of the 19th century, more Americans lived on farms than in cities. Now things were beginning to change in the North, where more than 20 million people lived. The cities were growing. Nearly 300,000 European immigrants a year flooded into the country through northern ports. Most were poor and stayed in these cities, taking any work they could find. One reason slavery had died out in the North was that immigrants provided cheap labor for the growing number of factories mass-producing goods such as clothes and shoes.

In the South, there were fewer than 10 million people—and nearly 4 million of those were salves. While most white South-erners made their living on small poor farms, a minority of rich landowners bought slaves to work their vast plantations. Tobacco, rice, and indigo had once been the major crops. Then, in 1793, Eli Whitney invented a machine called the cotton gin. This machine could easily separate cotton from its seeds. Suddenly cotton was being planted all over the South. Cotton mills in the North and in Europe bought up all the cotton they could find. Cotton became King—and the South became almost a one-crop economy.

Picking cotton was backbreaking work. Many field hands were needed to plant, grow, and harvest the crop. Most colonial Americans had believed that slavery would soon die out in the United States, a country founded on the ideas of freedom and liberty. Now, with the boom in cotton, slaves were once again in demand. In the 1850s, a good strong slave could cost as much as $1,800—more than Barton earned in a year at her good job in the Patent Office.

Harriet Beecher Stowe's book *Uncle Tom's Cabin,* published in 1852, helped rally more Northerners to the antislavery movement. Abolitionists wanted the government to end slavery everywhere. Southern politicians did not want "Yankees" telling them what to do.

The Northern states favored a strong central government. Southern states believed in *states' rights*—the right of the people in each state to make their own decisions within their own borders. Adding to the problem was the country's westward expansion. Both the North and the South wanted to spread their way of life—and their political ideas—into the new states and territories. For years these issues were debated in Congress. But the compro-mises—rules or plans to try to please everybody—all failed.

Southern states began to talk of their right to *secede*—to leave the Union and start their own nation. They believed the country was a union of *individual* states. Each state had joined by free choice. Each state had the freedom and the right to end its membership if it no longer believed in how the country was being run.

Northern states believed the Union was more important than any individual state. How could the country be strong if a state could just quit the Union any time it did not like a particular policy or law?

These differences grew into political battles and even violence. Emotions ran high. More and more, the North and South were like brothers and sisters fighting. The more one side criticized the other, the more that side angrily defended itself. The more they fought, the more each side covered its ears to any other point of view.

Slavery and states' rights were two important issues in the 1856 presidential election. Barton sided with the antislavery views of the Republican candidate John C. Frémont. He lost to James Buchanan. Barton and others worried: Would they be able to keep their jobs? Barton's friend Congressman DeWitt was not re-elected. Then Mason resigned as head of the Patent Office. A month later, Barton was out of a job. Sadly she moved home to North Oxford.

The next few years were unhappy ones for Barton. Her father was in his eighties and in poor health. Her brother Stephen had moved to North Carolina to set up a lumber business. She enjoyed spending time with her other relatives and friends, but she needed something useful to do. She took painting lessons. She pieced together a quilt. She went to lectures. She meddled in the problems of nieces and nephews. She had offers to teach, but she did not want to tie herself down—even though she had no idea where to go instead.

Still, she kept a close eye on the politics of Washington. She was against slavery. Yet she, along with many others, felt the extreme actions of some abolitionists were wrong. In October 1859, abolitionist John Brown took over a federal arsenal at Harpers Ferry, Virginia. He tried to lead a slave uprising against slave owners. Many in the North cheered his actions as those of a hero. Barton did not. She thought such violence backfired—that it only made Southerners more afraid of change and more willing to fight for their way of life. She began to sense that the country was heading toward violent tragedy—and that there was no turning back.

In November 1860, Abraham Lincoln was elected president. He was a member of the young Republican party and was strongly against the expansion of slavery in the West. Some friends of Barton's helped her get a job in the Patent Office as a temporary copyist. It did not offer the same status or pay as her old job, but Barton was thrilled to be back in Washington, D.C.

She had no idea that fate was leading her to the greatest challenge of her life—and to the work that would make her famous for generations.

It was both an exciting and a frightening time to be in Washington. Lincoln's election was the last straw for those in the South who favored states' rights. The air in Washington was filled with questions and debate: What would happen next?

Harpers Ferry, Virginia, was the scene of abolitionist John Brown's uprising.

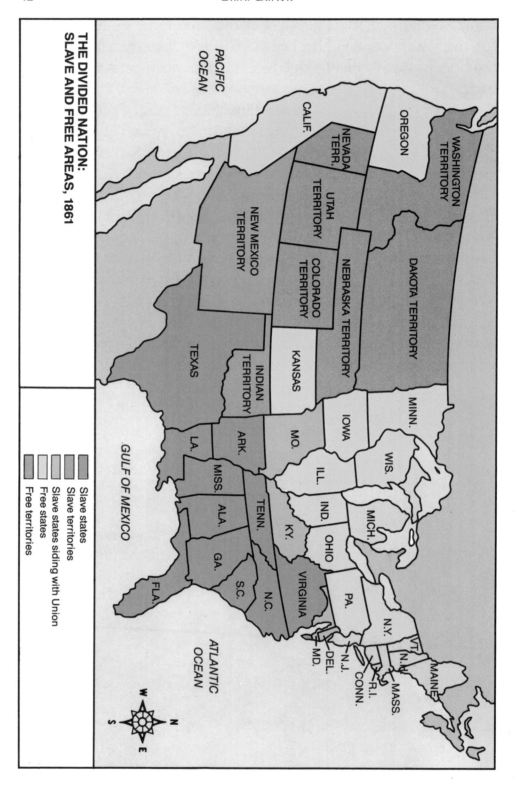

THE DIVIDED NATION:
SLAVE AND FREE AREAS, 1861

Slave states
Slave territories
Slave states siding with Union
Free states
Free territories

On December 20, 1860, South Carolina delegates met in Charleston, South Carolina, and took a vote that would change the course of American history. Every man there voted "Yes!" to secession: "The union now subsisting between South Carolina and other States, under the name of 'The United States of America,' is hereby dissolved." With these words they told the world that South Carolina was no longer a part of the United States. It would make its own laws. It would no longer answer to President Lincoln.

One by one, other Southern states voted to stand with South Carolina. In January and February, six more states seceded: Mississippi, Florida, Alabama, Georgia, Louisiana, and Texas. In late February, Southern delegates met in Montgomery, Alabama, and boldly declared themselves a new nation—the Confederate States of America. Though united under one government, each state would keep its "independent character." For president they chose Jefferson Davis, a former U.S. congressman, senator from Mississippi, and secretary of war.

Washington was in an uproar. Were the Southern rebels lawless traitors? Or were they spirited individuals bravely standing up for their beliefs? Had they really left the Union? Or were they putting on a daring show to force the government into compromise? The debates rang out from congressional chambers to bedchambers, from sewing rooms to barrooms.

There was fear, too, that Washington was not a safe place for the new president. The town was filled with Southerners. There had been threats to the president's life, and many feared he would not live to be inaugurated. To avoid trouble, Lincoln dressed in baggy old clothes and slipped into Washington from Illinois a day early.

A cold kept Barton home from the Inaugural Ball, but nothing could keep her from the inauguration itself. In a letter to Annie Childs, sister of her friend Fanny, Barton wrote: "The 4th of March has come and gone, and we have a *live Republican* President, and...during the whole day we saw no one who appeared to [show] the least dislike to his living...."

In his inaugural speech, President Lincoln declared the nation "unbroken." His stern message to the Southerners was that everything depended on what *they* chose to do. "In your hands, my dissatisfied fellow–countrymen, and not in *mine,* is the momentous issue of civil war. The government will not assail [attack] *you.* You can have no conflict, without being yourselves the aggressor."

For a while, nothing happened. Many did not believe the quarrel would actually come to war. But Lincoln had promised to protect all federal property in Southern territory, including Fort Sumter, on a small island off the coast of South Carolina. The Confederates could not put up with a "foreign" presence in such an important port. On April 12, 1861, Confederate President Jefferson Davis ordered General P.G.T. Beauregard to take the fort. After 34 hours, Major Robert Anderson surrendered the fort to the Confederates. No one was killed during the noisy battle, but the shots killed any hope of finding a peaceful end to the conflict.

The Civil War had begun. For the South, it was a fight for independence, for the right to make its own laws. For the North, it was a battle to preserve the Union. On both sides, good people were ready to stand up for their beliefs.

No one could yet imagine just how much every person's life would change. Not even Clara Barton.

THE WOULD-BE SOLDIER

"When there is no longer a soldier's arm to raise
the Stars and Stripes above our Capital, may
God give strength to mine."

CLARA BARTON, *Writing to
a friend about the coming war*

President Lincoln's answer to the attack on Fort Sumter was quick and clear. He called for 75,000 volunteers to help put down the Southern rebellion. A day later, thousands of men were heading toward Washington. Among the first was the Sixth Massachusetts Regiment, which included many of Barton's former students.

On April 19, the regiment stopped in Baltimore, Maryland, where they had to cross town to change trains. But Maryland was one of the "border states" between the North and the Deep South. The people's ties—and feelings—were mixed. Many people in Baltimore were in favor of Southern secession. They did not want Union troops in their town. An angry mob turned out to hoot and holler at the soldiers. Tempers flared. Shots were fired. Four soldiers and 12 civilians were killed, and 30 more were wounded, before the soldiers were able to leave on the train.

In Washington, there was nowhere to put so many soldiers, so they were housed in the Capitol building. Barton immediately went to tend to the wounded. She was shocked to hear that their baggage had been lost. Most were left with not so much as a handkerchief.

Here was an urgent need—and it spurred Barton to action.

First she emptied her own drawers to collect combs, buttons, scissors, and pens. The next day was Sunday. Shops were closed, but still she went to the merchants and bought supplies with her own savings. But there was something the young men needed even more: news. So Barton read aloud to them from their hometown newspaper, the *Worcester Spy.*

Barton had only begun. She put an ad in that same paper telling families and friends that they could send supplies to her. The response was overwhelming. Soon she became a one-woman warehouse for receiving and handing out the supplies.

Surprisingly, very little happened right away. Neither the North nor the South was prepared for war. No one seemed to know how to go about fighting it. Many leaders on both sides thought that one good battle or two would settle the whole matter.

Meanwhile, Barton used all her free time to visit the soldiers and gather the supplies they needed. Among the thousands of troops soon camped around the city, she found familiar faces—students from Bordentown, New Jersey, and other schools in which she had taught. Army food was terrible, so Barton brought them home-made jams and pies. Soldiers wrote home about Barton's kindness. Soon their wives and mothers began to send their goods to Clara Barton, knowing she would handle them with care and see them into the right hands.

Barton was kept busy and happy with this productive work. But these relatively peaceful early days of the war would soon be over. Then Barton would be faced with an even greater need.

On July 21, Union and Confederate soldiers met near Manassas, Virginia, about 25 miles from Washington. U.S. Brigadier General Irvin McDowell led a parade of soldiers toward the Southern troops of Brigadier General P.G.T. Beauregard, who were on the other side of a small river named Bull Run. Hundreds of men and women from Washington followed in buggies and on horseback. What a fine day to spread out a picnic on the hillside and watch the Union soldiers put the Rebels in their place! It was like a sports event. But when the men in these two untrained armies began to shoot each other, it was no game.

Battle plans fell apart. There were no "official" Union or Confederate uniforms yet. Many young men had made up their own hometown uniforms before joining. In the confusion, it was hard to tell who the enemy was. Untrained soldiers ignored orders or forgot what to do as real bullets whizzed round them.

At first, it seemed Union soldiers might break through the Confederate line and head straight for Richmond. Some of the Southerners began to retreat. Then their general saw a group of Virginia soldiers, led by Brigadier General Thomas J. Jackson, bravely holding the line. "There is Jackson standing like a stone wall!" the general cried. "Rally behind the Virginians!" The man who would soon be known as "Stonewall" Jackson had renewed the Rebels' will to fight. Soon they had Union soldiers on the run.

Back on a hillside, the picnickers watched in surprise as they saw their army running from the battlefield. Soldiers and civilians turned into a panic-stricken mob as they fled to Washington.

Washington was not prepared to handle the wounded. Nearly 3,000 Northern soldiers were killed, wounded, or missing from this one day of fighting. Makeshift hospitals were set up all around the city. Barton immediately went to help nurse the wounded.

Barton and many others that day saw that *this* was the reality of war—not the proud flags and the grand speeches. Suddenly the Battle of Bull Run (known in the South as the First Battle of Manassas) had changed everything. Perhaps for the first time, people in the North saw that Confederate independence could really happen.

Now Barton worked even harder to get basic supplies for these men: clean cotton clothing, canned fruits, soap. Within three months, she had filled three rented warehouses. Over the next year, as other battles brought more wounded, she went out to meet the arriving trains to care for the men as soon as she could.

Barton was shocked by their stories of the battlefield. Medicine, food, and clothing were carried to the front in slow-moving horse-drawn wagons that often took days to catch up with the army. Overworked surgeons treated only the most serious cases. Wounds became infected as soldiers lay on the ground waiting for help. Many bled to death in rough wagon rides back to the hospitals.

Lacking proper care, wounded soldiers—like these at Chancellorsville—could only despair.

Inspired by the relief work of her Washington landlady and friend, Almira Fales, Barton began to see that these wounded men needed help sooner. They needed food and first aid as soon as they could be dragged from battle.

It was a milestone in Barton's life. Though she could not yet know it, so many events of her youth had prepared her for this moment: the patriotic military stories and lessons at her father's knee; the fearless adventures with her cousins and her wild, free horseback lessons with David; her New England upbringing of thrift, hard work, and independence; her experience nursing her brother Stephen and the victims of smallpox.

There was also her frustration when told she could not do something just because she was a woman. There were her depressions, which seemed to lift only when she was being truly useful. And there was her constant need for praise.

These strengths and flaws made Barton the kind of woman who would find her own way to help fight this war. If she could not be a soldier, she would care for and support the young men who could. But she would not work in safety far from all the fighting. She would go where she could do the most good: to the battlefield itself.

This was a shocking idea in the 1860s, and far easier said than done. Women rarely went anywhere unescorted. It was hardly proper for decent women to go alone among rough soldiers in the midst of a bloody battlefield. Women who did were often the subject of gossip and considered indecent.

At the beginning of the Civil War, nursing was still considered a lowly, menial task. It was a dangerous, poorly paid job, filled by men, or by lower-class and immigrant women. There were no nursing schools; the work was simply learned on the job. Middle- and upper-class women could nurse their own families, but it was not proper for them to work for pay in a hospital nursing strangers.

One upper-class English woman named Florence Nightingale, however, had begun working to change these ideas. Several years earlier, in the 1854 conflict called the Crimean War, Turkey, Britain, and France fought with Russia over Turkey's independence. Reports of hospital conditions were horrible. Nightingale organized a group of 38 well-trained women nurses and got permission to go to the army hospitals. She treated thousands of wounded. She fought for clean hospitals and healthful food. She insisted that records be kept.

In only a few months, Nightingale helped lower the death rate in military hospitals from 42 percent to 2 percent. "The very first requirement in a hospital," she said, "must be that it should do the sick no harm." In 1860, she opened the first school of nursing, in St. Thomas's Hospital in London, England. Nightingale was the founder of modern nursing, and her work helped make nursing a respected profession.

Nightingale inspired many American women to volunteer as nurses during the Civil War. But attitudes did not change overnight. Often army officers and male doctors did not want their help.

Barton wrote to the War Department for passes to the front. She asked her political friends for help. Most government officials believed it was improper for women to go to the front. They thought women would get hysterical when they came face to face with real fighting. They would only be in the way.

Barton would not give up. In February 1862, she went home to North Oxford to be with her father, who at age 88 was dying. They had long talks about the war. She told him of her idea to go to the battlefield. Once Stephen Barton had forbidden his daughter to learn to skate because it was "not proper." But that was in the past. Now he told her to follow her heart.

Still, it was a daring choice even for the 40-year-old unmarried Barton. All her life she had dared to run beside the boys, and yet she feared the disapproval it often won her from society. Years after the war she admitted, "I struggled long and hard with my sense of propriety...I am ashamed that I thought of such a thing."

Like Barton, most of the middle-class and upper-class women in both the North and South who chose to serve struggled with their sense of what was "proper." Barton was lucky—her family was behind her. Many women had to fight rejection from family and friends. But every woman who risked her own reputation to do what she felt was right helped to lead all women past the prejudices of society. Their brave work during the Civil War surprised the nation. It added strength to the growing movement for women's rights.

From North Oxford, Barton wrote to Massachusetts Governor John A. Andrew for his permission to go to the front. In her letter she said: "If I know my own heart, I have none but right motives. I ask neither pay nor praises, simply a soldier's fare and the sanction [official permission] of Your Excellency to go and do with my might, whatever my hands find to do." The governor said he would help her, but the federal officials denied her requests.

On March 21, 1862, Barton's father died. Soon after, she returned to Washington and her work of gathering supplies. She used all her contacts in Washington to continue her appeal to go to the front. In July, she visited Colonel Daniel H. Rucker, assistant quartermaster, in charge of supplies. His noisy office was filled with the relatives of soldiers who had come to complain or ask for favors. When Rucker finally spoke to Barton, she burst into tears. At last she told him she wanted to go to the front.

Rucker started to tell her that the battlefield was no place for a lady. Suddenly her tears were gone. She told him she had three warehouses full of medical supplies and food to hand out. Immediately Rucker was won over. Within 24 hours Clara Barton got the permission she had sought for so long.

It had been a long wait. But Barton did not rush to the front with a wagonload of supplies. She had plans to make if her work was to succeed. First she traveled to New Jersey and New England to set up a system of getting supplies to Washington. She wrote: "People talk like children about 'transporting supplies' as if it were the easiest thing imaginable to transport supplies by wagon thirty miles across a country scouted by guerrilla bands."

Then, on August 9, came news of a battle at Cedar Mountain, near Culpepper, Virginia. Stonewall Jackson and 25,000 Confederate soldiers had crushed Union soldiers led by John Pope. Barton decided she was needed there. At last it was time to go to the front. What she wrote about this major event in her life shows a mixture of emotions. She was still worrying about what "society" thought of her work and felt compelled to defend it. But she also could not help but brag a little about what she had done.

> When our armies fought on Cedar Mountain, I broke the shackles and went to the field. Five days and nights with three hours' sleep— a narrow escape from capture—and some days of getting the wounded into hospitals at Washington brought Saturday, August 30. And if you chance to feel that the positions I occupied were rough and unseemly for a *woman*—I can only reply that they were rough and unseemly for *men*. But under all, lay the life of the Nation. I had inherited the rich blessing of health and strength of constitution—such as are seldom given to woman—and I felt that some return was due from me and that I ought to be there.

Union casualties were high: 314 killed, 1465 wounded, more than 600 missing. It took Barton four days to reach the battlefield, but wounded sailors still lay untreated on the crowded floors of hospitals and homes.

Dr. James Dunn, a Pennsylvania surgeon who witnessed her tireless work, wrote to his wife, "At the time when we were entirely out of dressings of every kind, she supplied us with everything, and while the shells were bursting in every direction...she staid [sic] dealing out shirts...and preparing soup and seeing it prepared in all the hospitals....I thought that night if heaven ever sent out a homely angel, she must be one her assistance was so timely."

Dunn was embarrassed when his letter found its way into the newspapers. He later wrote, "The letter was not written for publication, and I was much surprised to see it in print," and added, "The only untruth it contained was in saying that she was 'homely' for no one can be called so who is so truly good." Barton must have been embarrassed by it, too. In the clippings she kept, she marked through the word *homely* and wrote in *holy*.

In the 1860s, with no television or radio, people received their news of the war through newspapers or word of mouth. News was often slow in coming, and reports were often conflicting or unclear. As is common in any war, the news was often used to keep up morale. The papers were filled with stories of patriotism and glory.

To come face to face with the reality of war—the blood, the suffering, the mutilation and death—was overwhelming. But while nursing her brother David, Barton had learned to look past the blood and the often repulsive work she must do. Instead, she focused on the relief and gratitude she could bring to her patient's face. The military knowledge she had learned through her father's war stories and games gave her a steadier footing on the battlefield than many of the green, poorly trained soldiers. What she did not know, she learned as she labored. She would become a familiar face on the battlefields.

On August 31, 1862, she arrived by army wagon at the Second Battle of Bull Run, known in the South as Second Manassas. She described the scene later in a letter to a friend:

"The ground, for acres, was a thinly wooded slope—and among the trees, on the leaves and grass, were laid the wounded who were pouring in by scores of wagon loads, as picked up on the field under the flag of truce. All day they came, and the whole hillside was covered. Bales of hay were broken open and scattered over the ground like littering for cattle, and the sore, [starving] men were laid upon it.

"And when the night shut in, in the mist and darkness about us, we knew that...we were a little band of almost empty-handed workers literally by ourselves in the wild woods of Virginia, with three thousand suffering men crowded upon the few acres within our reach.

"After gathering up every available [tool] or convenience for our work, our domestic inventory stood, two water buckets, five tin cups, one camp kettle, one stewpan, two lanterns, four bread knives, three plates, and a two-quart tin dish, and three thousand guests to serve...."

In minutes they were preparing food and dressing wounds.

Countless wives, mothers, and daughters back home sent Barton precious supplies, including hundreds of boxes of homemade fruit preserves. "Every can, jar, bucket, bowl, cup or tumbler, when emptied, that instant became a vehicle of mercy to convey some preparation of mingled bread and wine or soup or coffee to some helpless, [starving] sufferer.... I never realized until that day how little a human being could be grateful for."

With candles in hand, Barton and a few helpers, including Almira Fales, worked without rest through the long, dark night. The men lay so close on the hay, it was difficult to walk without stepping on wounded arms or legs. Barton feared that any minute a dropped candle would set the whole hay-covered field of bodies on fire.

As they worked, the fighting continued. On Monday Clara wrote, "The enemy's cavalry appeared in the wood opposite and a raid was hourly expected. In the afternoon all the wounded men were sent off and the danger became so imminent [close at hand] that Mrs. Fales thought best to leave, although I begged to be excused from accompanying her, as the ambulances were up to the fields for more, and I knew I should never leave a wounded man there if I were taken prisoner forty times." Finally the last thousand wounded men were put on a train to Alexandria, where they arrived at 10 o'clock at night. "I had slept one and one half hours since Saturday night," Barton wrote, "and I am well and strong and wait to go again if I have need."

Barton had learned a great deal at Bull Run. The army's supplies and methods for getting them to the men were not filling the need. Brave young soldiers were dying needlessly for lack of a caring pair of hands. More than ever, Barton was sure of the importance of her work.

Soon after the Second Battle of Bull Run, Barton was at work among the wounded after the battle at Chantilly, Virginia. She worked without rest long into the night. At about three in the morning, a surgeon came with a candle to her. A young man was dying and calling for his sister. None could comfort him. Would she come?

Barton followed the surgeon. He warned her that the boy had been shot through the abdomen and would not last half an hour.

The Second Battle of Bull Run, shown in this drawing, saw 16,000 Union casualties.

Soon she came upon a group of men. By the light of their candles, she saw a young boy, bloody hands clutched at his chest, his eyes wild and searching. "Mary.... Don't let me die here alone...."

Barton motioned the others to step away with their lights. She knelt beside the boy in the darkness. Then she kissed his forehead and laid her cheek against his.

"Oh, Mary!" The boy cried out, clutching at her dress and hair. "I knew you would come if I called you.... Don't cry, Darling, I am not afraid to die now that you have come to me."

Barton sat on the ground and pulled the boy into her lap. She wrapped her own shawl about his shoulders. Soon he was asleep. And there she sat until dawn.

In the morning the boy awoke. He looked puzzled for a moment, then smiled. "I knew before I opened my eyes that this couldn't be Mary. I know now that she couldn't get here, but it is almost as good...."

The boy told Barton he was a poor woman's only son. He had promised her he would do whatever he could to make it home, dead or alive. He begged Barton for help.

The surgeon in charge of the train said there was room for only so many men. He did not want to waste a space on a soldier who was sure to die. Barton insisted the boy be given the chance, and at last the surgeon gave in. Not long after the battle, she learned that the boy had reached Washington, where he spent his last two days with his mother and his dear sister Mary.

It seemed to be a talent of Barton's: to do so much for so many, and still find time to tend the special needs of a single soldier.

Hundreds of wagons continued to bring the wounded in from the battle, only two miles away. The men were starving. Many were suffering from loss of blood. It would be at least 24 hours before the trains could get them to a real hospital. Though the fighting was moving closer, Barton felt that each soldier must be fed and his wounds tended to before he risked the long journey.

At three o'clock, the last of the wounded were carried away by train. At four, thunder and lightning ripped the sky and a hard rain began to fall. They could hear the battle coming closer. Another shipment of wounded arrived. That night, when the train took the last of the wounded away, Barton headed through the rain for a small tent that had been set up for her. "A well-established brook" was running through it. It was Monday night. She had not eaten or slept since Saturday. So she sank down in the middle of the water, propped her head on her hand, and went to sleep—despite her fear that she would wake up with water flowing into her ears.

The morning of the third day found a drenched, hungry, exhausted army in retreat. The hills were filled with Southern cavalry. But Barton would not leave as long as there were wounded to treat. At three o'clock, a Union officer rode up beside her.

"Miss Barton, can you ride?"

"Yes, sir," she replied.

"Then you can risk another hour," he said before riding off.

At four, the officer galloped up and leaped from his horse.

"Now is your time," he exclaimed. "The enemy is already breaking over the hills."

In two minutes Clara Barton—and the last of the wounded— were safely on the train heading for Washington.

WOMEN IN THE CIVIL WAR

"All nurses are required to be plain-looking
women...."

FROM DOROTHEA DIX'S REQUIREMENTS
FOR ARMY NURSE VOLUNTEERS

T hroughout the war, Clara Barton often cooperated with many individuals and organizations. But she believed she could do more good if she was free to go where she saw the greatest need. She also craved the praise and attention her work brought her. She did not like to share her successes, whether at the Bordentown school or at the Battle of Bull Run. Barton often had two or three other women working with her at the front. But when she wrote accounts of the battles and her work, she sometimes did not give the other women's names. Barton could organize and give orders, but she was not good at taking them. Whenever possible, she worked alone.

Many other women in the war, however, worked through more organized channels.

Elizabeth Blackwell, the first American woman doctor, was one of the first to organize women volunteers. She was a leader in creating the Women's Central Association for Relief (WCAR), which, among other things, set up training programs for nurses. This became the foundation for the United States Sanitary Commission, made up of men and women, which hoped to organize relief efforts in the North. The commission created a system for distributing supplies fairly among the troops. It raised millions of dollars through fundraising bazaars called "Sanitary Fairs." Like Florence Nightingale, the commission fought to improve the unsanitary conditions found in military hospitals and at the front. Other relief agencies included the Western Sanitary Commission, and the Christian Commission, formed by YMCA members, which took food, medicine, and religion to the soldiers in the field.

At the start of the war, as Barton's favored Sixth Massachusetts Regiment poured into Washington, 59-year-old Dorothea Lynn Dix was also in the capital to volunteer. Like Barton, she had been a young unmarried woman in Massachusetts, unsure of her calling. She, too, had taught poor children in a free school. Then one day in 1841, she accepted a volunteer teaching job that would change her life: teaching Sunday school in a Massachusetts jail for women. She discovered that many of the prisoners were in fact mentally ill. They were treated like animals and locked away in crowded, filthy cells, unhelped and forgotten.

Dorothea Dix had found her life's work. She spent two years visiting every jail, hospital, and poorhouse she could in Massachusetts. She took detailed notes on how the mentally ill were treated. Many prisoners were bound in chains, beaten, and tortured into submission. She then embarked on an "unfeminine" career of public service, waging battle in statehouses across the nation to establish publicly-funded hospitals for the humane treatment of the country's thousands of mentally ill. Her reform work brought her much publicity and taught her a great deal about politics.

When war broke out, Dix brought her skills and passion to Washington. On June 10, 1861, she was appointed Superintendent of Women Nurses.

At once she threw herself into her work with the fiery conviction of a reformer. She organized infirmaries in Washington. She interviewed and supervised nurses and collected medical supplies. She even wrote procedures for women back home on how to set up sewing societies. But her methods and her attitudes were highly controversial and won her few friends.

Dorothea Dix reformed treatment of the mentally ill before organizing nursing during the Civil War.

Like Nightingale, Dix sought to raise the standards of nursing. In this emotional, patriotic war, many young women volunteered for service out of a romantic sense of adventure. They could not imagine the reality of the work before them. Others were bored at home, with the men gone and social activities canceled. Perhaps others hoped to find a husband among the men before becoming an "old maid."

TO CARE FOR THE WOUNDED

Medical knowledge advanced little between the Middle Ages and the U.S. Civil War. When war broke out doctors had no understanding of bacteria and the importance of hygiene. Surgical equipment was not sterilized. Vermin swarmed in every camp, and diseases swept through whole divisions at a time, leaving death and disfigurement. On both sides, more soldiers died of disease and infection than from enemy bullets. Some anesthetics were used in surgery, but often a shot of whiskey was all a soldier got before his arm or leg was cut off. A handful of brave and determined people fought against these inhuman conditions. The U.S. Sanitary Commission and the Christian Commission helped improve standards of cleanliness and brought food, medicine and bandages to the camps. Mary Ann Bickerdyke was busily setting up nursing operations at an Illinois army camp when General Ulysses Grant heard about her talents. With his cooperation, she became the head of nursing for the western armies, establishing more than 300 field hospitals. The grateful soldiers dubbed her "Mother Bickerdyke."

In this photo taken at Gettysburg, a doctor is about to amputate a soldier's leg.

The U.S. Sanitary Commission pushed for a trained ambulance corps to replace amateurs who often fled battle.

"Mother Bickerdyke" brought hygiene and a healing spirit to the armies of generals Grant and Sherman.

These were not the women Dorothea Dix wanted to work for her. She wanted serious women who wound not faint at the sight of blood or turn up their noses at the dirty chores they would face in an army hospital. Because of society's attitudes, women nurses could easily become the subject of crude jokes and gossip. In an age when both men and women rarely went out unless they were dressed from head to toe, these nurses would see many "indelicate" things as they helped nurse the undressed bodies of strange wounded men.

Dix issued strict orders: "No woman under 30 need apply to serve in government hospitals. All nurses are required to be plain-looking women. Their dresses must be brown or black, with no bows, no curls, no jewelry, and no hoop skirts." Once accepted, the nurses were subject to her continued control and discipline.

In the South, relief efforts were far less organized. The people were poorer and more spread-out. Still, here, as in the North, volunteers worked long and hard. "We had no Sanitary Commission in the South," wrote one Southerner, "we were too poor.... With us each house was a hospital." Sally Louisa Thompkins started a hospital in Richmond and was the only woman ever commissioned by the Confederacy. Phoebe Levy Pember, known for her work in organizing hospitals, was first matron at Chimborazo Hospital in Richmond, which was then one of the largest military hospitals in the world. Hundreds of unnamed women also "broke the rules" of society and served as nurses throughout the South. Many went first to a hospital to nurse a husband or son, then stayed on to help hundreds of others when they saw how much they were needed.

On both sides of the war, more than twice as many men died from disease and untreated wounds as died from a bullet in battle. Infectious diseases spread quickly through every military camp. Most people in the mid-1800s had grown up and lived in one place. When war broke out, hundreds of young men were suddenly thrown together in unsanitary conditions and exposed to all kinds of new illnesses. Diseases such as measles, smallpox, dysentery, and typhoid fever spread like wildfire.

Medicine was still in the dark ages. People did not yet understand what caused infection. No one had discovered that it was caused by bacteria. After working on one patient, a doctor might rinse his hands and operating instruments in a bucket of creek water before turning to the next patient. Nearly every wound became infected, and there were no antibiotics to cure the infection.

Amputations were common—Barton's diary entries and letters often mention "piles" of amputated arms and legs—and were done with only ether or chloroform to ease the pain. When these ran out, many a soldier literally had to "bite the bullet" as he faced amputation with nothing but a slug of whiskey in him.

Surgeons and other medical workers were in short supply. There were not enough hospitals to take care of the wounded, so they were often treated in schools, churches, factories, and homes.

But from this spectacle of sickness and death, a positive change was born. As more and more men fell in battle, other men were needed to fill their empty places in the army. Just when doctors had more patients to treat, they found themselves with fewer male aides to help them. Women moved into these nursing roles and proved that they could get the work done. Some doctors even began to prefer women nurses.

The work done by women such as Barton, Dix, Tompkins, Pember, and thousands of other "unsung heroes" throughout the North and South earned women new respect and admiration. Their dedication helped change society's view of women as "the weaker sex."

CORNMEAL AND CANDLES

"Our army was weary, and lacked not only
physical strength, but confidence and spirit. And
why should they not? Always defeated! Always
on the retreat! I was almost demoralized myself!
And I had just commenced."

CLARA BARTON, *On seeing stragglers on her way to the*
Battle of Antietam

I t was September 1862. The war that all had thought would
be over in months had turned into a war that seemed to
have no end. In battle after battle, the Union army suffered
nothing but defeat.

Most of the battles had been fought on Southern land, but that
was about to change. After a string of successes, Confederate
General Robert E. Lee decided to make his first move into
Northern territory. He felt the South's best chance for ending the
war was to bring the fighting into the North's "front yard." He
believed the war-weary Northerners would decide it was not worth
it to keep fighting. Let those Rebels go off and start their own
country if they wanted to—and good riddance! Lee also hoped a
success here would win Europe's recognition of the Confederate
government.

In September, Robert E. Lee and Stonewall Jackson headed for
Maryland, where Barton's Sixth Massachusetts Regiment had been
attacked. Though Maryland was a slave state, it had stayed in the
Union. Its people were divided. Many still felt strong ties with the

South. Lee hoped his bold strike here would give Marylanders the courage to join the Confederate cause.

Clara Barton received secret advance information. With only a driver and a few men, she rode by wagon over the hills of Maryland, then camped that night in an open field. The sound of distant gunfire interrupted their sleep. Before daybreak, they were lumbering along with a 10-mile train of army supply wagons.

By the time they reached Harpers Ferry, the battle was over. "There, where we now walked with peaceful feet, twelve hours before the ground had rocked with carnage.... And there, side by side, stark and cold in death mingled the Northern Blue and Southern Gray."

Barton hurried on and caught up with the wagon train of army supplies. She became frustrated traveling behind the long line of wagons. Ammunition wagons always went first, in case there was a battle. Then came food and clothing, and finally the medical

supplies. Barton decided that something must be done to gain time. Her new motto was "Follow the cannon!"

She and her men camped early and slept. At one o'clock in the morning, they rode out and passed the whole train, which was still camping for the night. By daybreak, they had caught up with the cannon at the front of the line. At nightfall, they came upon General Ambrose E. Burnside and his Army of the Potomac. More than 80,000 men awaited battle along Antietam Creek, near Sharpsburg, Maryland.

"In all this vast assemblage I saw no other trace of womankind. I was faint, but could not eat; weary, but could not sleep; depressed, but could not weep." Barton climbed into her wagon and prayed for Union victory.

The next morning, September 16, Barton watched the beginning of the distant battle through field glasses. She saw cavalry and artillery being sent to support forces in danger of being attacked. *That* was where she wanted to be. She and her aides followed the troops for eight miles till they came to a cornfield near a house and barn. Already the yard was littered with wounded men.

Barton filled her arms with bandages and medicines and headed toward the house. At the gate she met one of the surgeons, and for a moment he was speechless.

"God indeed has remembered us!" he cried. "How did you get here so soon?"

The surgeons had nothing but the few instruments and packets of ether they had brought themselves. Every sheet in the house had been torn up for bandages. On the porch the surgeons were busy operating on four plain wooden tables—with nothing but green corn husks to bind the wounds.

Barton worked on through the day with never a rest, in the smoke of battle that was so thick it was almost impossible to see.

A soldier lying on the ground asked for water, and Barton bent to help him. "Just at this moment a bullet sped its free and easy way between us, tearing a hole between us, tearing a hole in my sleeve and found its way into his body. He fell back dead. There was no more to be done for him and I left him to rest. I have never mended

Photographer Mathew Brady took this portrait of Barton at the height of her Civil War efforts.

that hole in my sleeve. I wonder if a soldier ever does mend a bullet hole in his coat?"

Just outside the barn, one soldier cried, "Lady, will you tell me what this is that burns so?" The man held his fingers to his wounded face. Barton told him that he had a bullet lodged in his cheekbone.

"It is terribly painful," he said. "Won't you take it out?" Barton turned to fetch a surgeon, but the young man grabbed her skirts. "No! They cannot come to me. I must wait my turn, for this is a little wound. Please take the ball out for me."

"I had never severed the nerves and fibers of human flesh," Barton remembered, "and I said I could not hurt him so much."

"You cannot hurt me, dear lady," the man said. "I can endure any pain that your hands can create."

Barton could not say no. She pulled out her pocket knife and prepared for the operation. Nearby, a sergeant who had been shot through both thighs lay watching. "I will help do that," he said with a smile. Slowly he dragged his torn body beside her. While he gently held the man's head in his hands, Barton removed the bullet.

"I do not think a surgeon would have pronounced it a scientific operation," recalled Barton, "but that it was successful I dared to hope from the gratitude of the patient."

At two o'clock, one of Barton's helpers brought word that all the food she had brought was gone. Only three boxes of wine were left.

"Open the wine and give that," said Barton, "and God help us."

The man opened a box and cried out with surprise. The women back home had packed the wine not in sawdust—but in cornmeal!

Barton searched the farmhouse and found six huge kettles. Soon she was cooking up gallons of cornmeal gruel. All night she and several men carried buckets of the life-giving food to the wounded, wherever they fell.

Late that night, Barton went into the farmhouse and found the head surgeon staring at the stub of a tallow candle.

"You look tired," Barton said to him.

"Tired!" he cried. "Yes, I am tired, tired of such heartlessness, such carelessness!....Here are at least one thousand wounded men, terribly wounded, five hundred of whom cannot live till daylight, without attention. That two inches of candle is all I have or can get. What can I do? How can I endure it?"

Barton led him to the door and pointed toward the barn. Lanterns hung inside and out.

"What is that?" he exclaimed.

"The barn is lighted," Barton said, "and the house will be directly."

"Who did it?"

At the Battle of Antietam, one of the bloodiest of the war, Clara Barton eased the suffering.

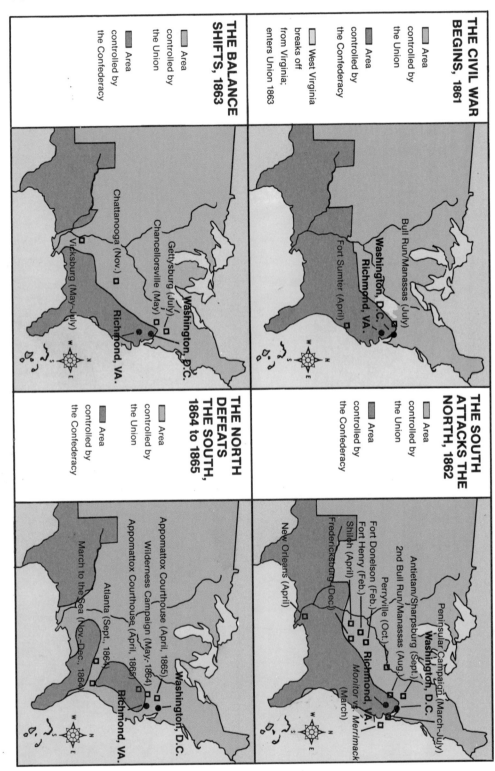

THE CIVIL WAR BEGINS, 1861

☐ West Virginia breaks off from Virginia; enters Union 1863

▨ Area controlled by the Confederacy

▢ Area controlled by the Union

THE BALANCE SHIFTS, 1863

▢ Area controlled by the Union

▨ Area controlled by the Confederacy

Chattanooga (Nov.)
Vicksburg (May–July)
Gettysburg (July)
Chancellorsville (May)
Washington, D.C.
Richmond, VA.

THE SOUTH ATTACKS THE NORTH, 1862

▢ Area controlled by the Union

▨ Area controlled by the Confederacy

Bull Run/Manassas (July)
Washington, D.C.
Richmond, VA.
Fort Sumter (April)

THE NORTH DEFEATS THE SOUTH, 1864 to 1865

▢ Area controlled by the Union

▨ Area controlled by the Confederacy

Appomattox Courthouse (April, 1865)
Wilderness Campaign (May, 1864)
Appomattox Courthouse (April, 1865)
Atlanta (Sept., 1864)
March to the Sea (Nov.–Dec., 1864)
Washington, D.C.
Richmond, VA.

Peninsular Campaign (March–July)
Antietam/Sharpsburg (Sept.)
2nd Bull Run/Manassas (Aug.)
Perryville (Oct.)
Fort Donelson (Feb.)
Fort Henry (Feb.)
Shiloh (April)
Fredericksburg (Dec.)
Washington, D.C.
Richmond, VA.
Monitor vs. Merrimack (March)
New Orleans (April)

"I, Doctor."

"Where did you get them?"

"Brought them with me."

"How many have you?"

"All you want—four boxes."

The surgeon stared at her for a long moment. With renewed energy, he hurried back to his work.

At dawn, a hush covered the hills. The Union army had ended Lee's strike into Northern territory, and his troops were retreating. But the losses on both sides were horrible. In one day of fighting, 12,410 Union soldiers and 13,724 Confederates had been killed.

Antietam was a turning point in the war. Lee's defeat lost him the European support he had hoped for. The North had a victory that would bring new energy to their fighting. With the Union basking in success, the president chose to change the tone of the war.

On September 22, 1862, Abraham Lincoln issued the Emancipation Proclamation: "That on the 1st day of January, A.D. 1863, all persons held as slaves within any State...in rebellion against the United States shall be then, thenceforth, and forever free." It was a strange document. With it, Lincoln freed the slaves in the rebellious Confederate states, where the federal government had no real power. But it did not free slaves in the states that were still part of the Union. Abolitionists were angry—they felt it did not go far enough. Many Northern politicians and army officers criticized it. Still, the Emancipation Proclamation did what Lincoln had hoped it would do: It rallied people to a new, moral cause. No longer was the war being fought mainly to preserve the Union. Now it was also a battle for freedom.

Of all of Clara Barton's war work, Antietam was perhaps her finest hour. Here her work was truly heroic, and here she won the admiration of the common soldiers and of many surgeons. She had proved her courage and ability beyond a doubt—to the army and to herself. She had marched with the soldiers, gone without food and rest, slept under the stars, and stood her ground under fire, even when others ran. She had lived the life of a soldier, and she had outdistanced many of the men.

From now on, Barton would hunger for the sights and sounds of the battlefield, and for new chances to show the world what a true soldier she could be.

GETTING THERE

"I will tell you how to become the most scientific little Box packer in the country."

CLARA BARTON, *In a letter to friend Mary Norton,*
September 26, 1862

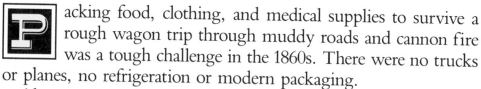

acking food, clothing, and medical supplies to survive a rough wagon trip through muddy roads and cannon fire was a tough challenge in the 1860s. There were no trucks or planes, no refrigeration or modern packaging.

Also, no one was prepared for the amount of food and supplies needed for thousands of sick, starving, dying men in a war that seemed never to end. There were no modern assembly lines or high-speed machinery to churn out urgently needed goods. Every piece of clothing, every jar of food was made—slowly—by hand. Nearly every woman in the nation became a producer, nearly every home a manufacturer of socks and shirts and home-canned fruit.

Clara Barton helped turn the preparation and packing of those goods into a fine art. She knew from first-hand experience that those supplies were priceless—and the loss of a single box of fruit or bandages could mean the difference between life and death.

From Washington, she wrote Mary Norton a 10-page letter on how to pack supplies so they would reach the battlefield in useful condition.

Do not make the packages too large, she recommended. Big boxes usually got rough treatment. Stewed foods were dangerous, since they might build up pressure on the bumpy trip and explode.

"Lemons are very nice," she wrote, "but best by [sic] the whole box—they keep much better before disturbing. —Soldiers eat them like apples, they get so little acid and crave it so, I have seen a wounded man clutch at a piece of lemon as a child does an orange."

Then there was her priceless lesson from Antietam: Pack fragile items in something useful, such as cornmeal or bran.

Label each box clearly and list each item packed inside, Barton wrote. Then she would not have to waste time opening it, but could sort her boxes quickly. "Knowledge is *time* you know—it used to be said that it was *money*, but it is a great deal more than that."

Barton had plenty of practical advice. But she also knew that special touches could boost a soldier's spirit—which was often as wounded as his body.

"Your pillows are a great luxury," she wrote in another letter to Mary. "How the poor fellows crave them." She had one important suggestion: Make the pillowcases out of old calico dresses. "If a calico case gets greasy and soiled, the man if able can take if off and soap and wash it, and replace it, and it will smell clean, and not look badly. A white case would be a perfect fright."

Though recovering from an illness, Barton continued her supply work in Washington. Still, she longed to be at the front again, where she felt she could do the most good. When fighting was reported in the Shenandoah Valley of Virginia, the army gave Barton 4 wagons and 8 to 10 men to transport supplies. They were not soldiers, but civilians employed by the government. They had been hardened by their months of work driving in the thick of battle. They were not happy to be heading back into the fighting— especially with a woman telling them what to do. They were rude to Barton. They stopped the wagons and made camp early, ignoring her plans.

Barton knew how to handle them. She used her own brand of discipline, which had worked in her unruly classrooms. She built a fire and cooked them a delicious supper. The men ate without a word.

Later that evening, the leader came to and spoke for the group: "We come to tell you we are ashamed of ourselves," he said. "The truth is, in the first place we didn't want to come. . . . and then we never saw a train under charge of a woman before and we couldn't understand it, and we didn't like it, and we've been mean and contrary all day, and said a good many hard things and you've treated us like gentlemen. We had no right to expect that supper from you, a better meal than we've had in two years. And you've been as polite to us as if we'd been the General and his staff, and it makes us ashamed. And we've come to ask your forgiveness."

Barton forgave them, and assured them that "as for my being a woman, they would get accustomed to that."

At field hospitals, Barton fought disorganization, which she claimed led to disease and death.

The next morning, Barton awoke to the sound of hushed voices and rattling dishes and the crackling of a fire. Minutes later, one of the men brought her a bucket of fresh water to wash up with and announced that her breakfast was ready.

"I had cooked my last meal for my drivers," said Barton. "These men remained with me six months through frost and snow and march and camp and battle; and nursed the sick, dressed the wounded, soothed the dying, and buried the dead; and if possible grew kinder and gentler every day."

THE FEARLESS SOLDIER

"Already the roll of the moving artillery is
sounding in my ears, the battle draws near, and I
must catch one hour's sleep for tomorrow's
labor."

CLARA BARTON, *In a letter written the night before the*
Battle of Fredericksburg

n December 1862, Barton got word of another battle. Soon she was stationed in Falmouth, Virginia, at the Lacy House, on the banks of the Rappahannock River. Across the river lay Fredericksburg, in the hands of the Confederates. Barton stood in the cold, icy wind and watched as General Ambrose Burnside's Union soldiers worked urgently to build pontoon bridges across the rain-swollen river.

Pontoons—flat wooden boats—were put in the water side by side. Wooden boards were nailed down on them to make a bridge. It had taken a week to get the pontoons by train, and work had been delayed. That gave General Robert E. Lee time to evacuate the Southern city and send for Stonewall Jackson to join him with more troops. Despite the odds, Burnside went ahead with his original plans, an action that became known as "Burnside's Blunder."

From every window and rooftop in Fredericksburg, Confederate snipers fired down on Union soldiers as they struggled to cross the river. At last, Union soldiers poured into the city.

At 10 o'clock, when the fighting had reached a peak, a Union soldier rushed up the steps of the Lacy House and placed a crumpled, bloody scrap of paper in Barton's hand. It was a note from a surgeon working inside the city: "Come to me. Your place is here."

Barton's wagon drivers tried to stop her. But soon she was making her way across the swaying pontoon bridge with gunshot flying all around her. On the other side, an officer reached up to help her down from the bridge. "While our hands were raised in the act of stepping down," Barton later wrote, "a piece of exploding shell hissed through between us, just below our arms, carrying away a portion of both the skirts of his coat and my dress." Undaunted, Barton hurried into the city to help the wounded. Less than half an hour later, the officer who had helped her was brought to her—dead.

Somehow Barton escaped injury, while 12,000 Union soldiers lost their lives. Every house became a hospital. Barton hurried from one to the next, tending the wounded.

The Battle of Fredericksburg was a total defeat for the Union army. Barton would never forget the images of the battle. "The wounded were brought to me, frozen, for days after.... The many wounded lay, uncared for, on the cold snow." The wounded were packed into every inch of space in the Lacy House, and blood covered the floors. Barton wrote that as she rose from tending to one soldier, "I wrung the blood from the bottom of my clothing, before I could step, for the weight about my feet."

To Barton and other relief workers, the scenes of death and destruction that filled Fredericksburg were foul and shameful. The noble causes of the war seemed to pale as the winter sun shone down on the broken bloody bodies of young men from both sides. Barton stayed on until the end of December as the last of the wounded were treated. In a letter to Annie Childs, she said she returned home to her rooms in Washington "cheerless, in confusion, and alone." Her mind was filled with "death scenes, never to be erased. The fires of Fredericksburg still blazed before my eyes, and her cannon still thundered at my ear.... and when, there

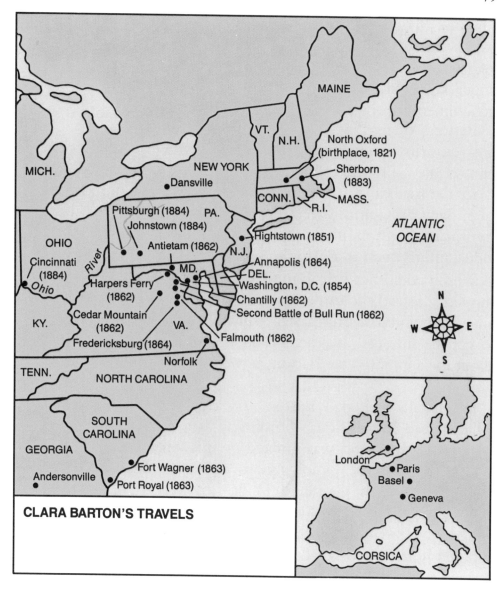

MAINE

VT.

N.H.

North Oxford
(birthplace, 1821)

Sherborn
(1883)

MICH.

NEW YORK

Dansville

CONN.

MASS.

R.I.

Pittsburgh (1884) PA.

Johnstown (1884)

Hightstown (1851)

OHIO

Antietam (1862)

N.J.

ATLANTIC
OCEAN

Cincinnati
(1884)

River

Ohio

Harpers Ferry
(1862)

MD.

Annapolis (1864)

DEL.

Washington, D.C. (1854)

Chantilly (1862)

Second Battle of Bull Run (1862)

KY.

Cedar Mountain
(1862)

VA.

Fredericksburg (1864)

Falmouth (1862)

Norfolk

TENN.

NORTH CAROLINA

SOUTH
CAROLINA

GEORGIA

Fort Wagner (1863)

Andersonville

Port Royal (1863)

N

W E

S

London

Paris

Basel

Geneva

CORSICA

CLARA BARTON'S TRAVELS

for the first time I looked at myself, shoeless, gloveless, ragged, and bloodstained, a new sense of desolation and pity and sympathy and weariness, all blended, swept over me with irresistible force....I sank down...and wept."

The war came nearly to a standstill as winter weather set in. Barton spent the time in Washington resting and building up supplies. She was nearly out of money, and the donations from volunteers were no longer enough. In January, she went to visit longtime friend Henry Wilson, one of Massachusetts's senators. She hoped he could use his political influence to help draw from the government's medical supplies.

Barton's own efforts, however, had actually led to changes in how the army ran its medical efforts. A new ambulance corps had been created. Procedures at army hospitals had improved. In late 1862, the medical department had at last given its support to the U.S. Sanitary Commission. The government hoped to gather all civilian relief efforts into this one organization—and reduce individual efforts such as Barton's.

Wilson could not help Barton win direct access to government supplies. Instead, he came up with a scheme to have her brother David appointed quartermaster, which would make it easier for her to get the supplies. Neither David nor his wife Julia was happy about the appointment. Barton, however, thought it was a perfect plan.

In May 1863, David Barton was assigned to Port Royal, on Hilton Head Island, South Carolina. Clara Barton applied to the War Department and was granted permission to follow. She was eager to arrive, for Union troops were planning an attack on Charleston, South Carolina, in an attempt to recapture Fort Sumter. She also hoped that as the army made its way inland, she might get to see her brother Stephen. At the start of the war, he had declared himself neutral and stayed in North Carolina rather than surrender his property to the Confederates. She had not heard from him in over a year.

Barton was thrilled when she arrived and learned the attack was to begin that very afternoon. Within a week, however, the attack "had fizzled." The bombardment of Charleston would drag on for eight months.

Meanwhile, a lively social group developed at Port Royal. Some of the officers had their wives with them, and there were teas and elegant dinners served on white linen tablecloths. It was quite a change from the life Barton had led the previous year.

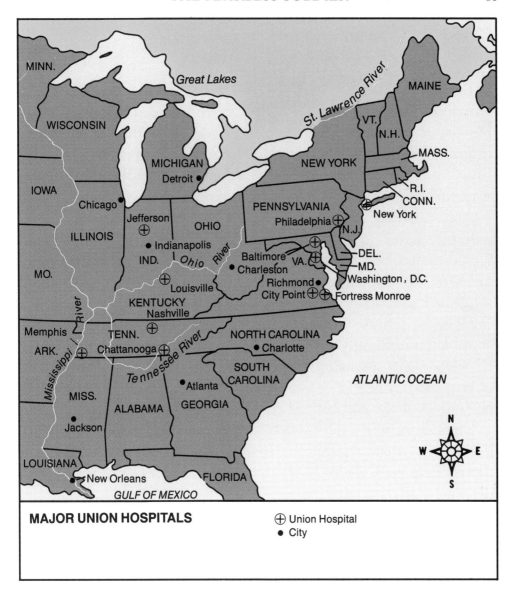

MINN.

Great Lakes

St. Lawrence River

MAINE

WISCONSIN

VT.

N.H.

MASS.

MICHIGAN

Detroit

NEW YORK

R.I.

CONN.

IOWA

Chicago

Jefferson

OHIO

PENNSYLVANIA

Philadelphia

New York

N.J.

ILLINOIS

Indianapolis

IND.

Ohio River

Baltimore

VA.

DEL.

MD.

MO.

Charleston

Richmond

Washington, D.C.

Louisville

City Point

Fortress Monroe

KENTUCKY

Nashville

Memphis

TENN.

Tennessee River

NORTH CAROLINA

ARK.

Chattanooga

Charlotte

SOUTH
CAROLINA

ATLANTIC OCEAN

Mississippi River

MISS.

Atlanta

ALABAMA

GEORGIA

Jackson

N

LOUISIANA

FLORIDA

W E

New Orleans

S

GULF OF MEXICO

MAJOR UNION HOSPITALS

⊕ Union Hospital
● City

Among the many interesting people at Port Royal were Captain Samuel T. Lamb, son of the Barton family's doctor, and Colonel John J. Elwell, of Cleveland, Ohio, the chief quartermaster of the Department of the South. Captain Lamb and Colonel Elwell showered Barton with flowers and invitations to go horseback riding, and at 41 she felt like a young girl again. Soon, however, Barton began to feel guilty about being so comfortable while soldiers continued to suffer on the battlefield. Her friends advised her to stay, though, including Colonel Elwell, who had become a close friend and admirer.

Barton found Colonel Elwell intelligent and gentle. It was wonderful to spend time with a man who treated her as an equal. He shared her love of horseback riding, and they spent many mornings riding along the island beaches. Despite the fact that Elwell had a wife at home in Ohio, their friendship grew into a wartime romance. Elwell often spoke of their future together. Barton, however, seemed to know it could not last.

In July, news came of a horrible three-day battle in Pennsylvania. Confederate General Robert E. Lee had once again tried to move the war into Northern territory. His plans fell apart, however, when he lost touch with his scout, cavalry leader J.E.B. Stuart, the "eyes of the army." With no information on the enemy, Lee's army stumbled unwillingly into battle with the Union's General George C. Meade near a small village called Gettysburg. After three days of horrible fighting, Lee was forced to retreat. Many saw it as the beginning of the end for his Army of Northern Virginia.

Gettsyburg was the bloodiest battle of the war so far: The North lost 23,000 men, the South, more than 28,000. Barton felt she should have been there. More than ever, she felt out of touch with the war.

Soon after, Barton learned that Hilton Head's General Quincy A. Gillmore was planning to take over Confederate Fort Wagner on Morris Island 75 miles away. Once again, Barton jumped at the chance to serve at the scene of battle. During the week-long siege, she tended to the wounded whom the overworked surgeons did not have time to treat. Union troops at last took Fort Wagner, then used it to step up the attack on Charleston. Barton pitched her tent on the sands of Morris Island and began to nurse and feed the wounded.

Food and medical supplies soon ran low. Barton was constantly begging army medical officials for supplies and complaining about the army's poor treatment of soldiers. Tired of her criticism, they actively opposed her work and tried to force her off the island. The

The Christian Commission brought food and medicine to soldiers in the field.

feud grew so bitter, Barton at last broke down both physically and emotionally, as she had during the quarrels at her old Bordentown school. She lost her voice and had trouble with her eyes. Her nerves were worn out, and she was severely depressed. For two weeks, Elwell and other friends tried to help her feel better again.

After all she had done in the war, this rejection stunned her. She saw no place for herself with the Sanitary Commission and Dorothea Dix's nurses, who were now handling most relief work in the area. She became defensive, and her empty hours were filled with feelings of self-doubt and frustration.

Perhaps the one thing that saved Barton from total depression that fall was a new friendship with Frances Dana Gage. Gage was an active feminist and abolitionist who wrote a column in *The Ohio Cultivator* under the pseudonym Aunt Fanny. Like Barton, she had grown up somewhat of a tomboy with liberal ideas. In 1862, she had left her husband and seven of her eight children and had come to the islands to help abandoned slaves work one of the contraband plantations. Barton saw the practical problems facing freed slaves, who owned nothing, had been denied an education, and must now start a new life. Barton worked with her and helped teach some of the blacks to read. More and more, Barton spoke out on the rights of blacks. She began to share Gage's belief that the horrors of the Civil War were God's punishment for the slavery in the South.

Barton and Gage became good friends. They shared a love of literature, and both dabbled in writing poetry. Both were passionate humanitarians. Gage also inspired Barton's growing political feelings about women's rights. Barton had never before been an active feminist. She had suffered prejudice—and fought it—on a personal level. Gage convinced Barton that the individual woman could only win true respect when she helped secure equal rights for *all* women.

Despite this new friendship, Barton grew frustrated with no major work to fill her hours. David received a letter from Stephen, saying that he was well, but that he felt it was safest to stay where he was until the war was over. David was in such poor health that he had to leave the army. Barton's romance with Colonel Elwell had cooled. In January of 1864, she went back to Washington.

Barton found little happiness there, either. The Sanitary and Christian Commissions were doing a well-organized job of gathering and distributing supplies. Having been away from Washington for a year, she had trouble getting passes to go to the front. That winter, Barton sank into a deep depression. She wrote self-pitying letters to old friends. Some days she could not even get out of bed.

Spring, however, gave birth to a new stage of the war. General Ulysses S. Grant, who had had much success in the West, was

General Sherman's men destroyed tracks, bridges, and roads on their devastating march to the sea.

given command of Northern troops in the East. General Robert E. Lee's Southern army was running out of everything—food, boots, bullets, even men. Yet they still had a psychological advantage: they were fighting to defend their home soil. They were fighting for independence. The Union, on the other hand, had the advantage of a larger population, most of the country's factories, and a better railroad. Grant's strategy was one of persistence: He would never retreat, even if the cost in men was high. He would attack the enemy again and again until they simply gave up.

In May 1864, Grant began a march toward the Confederate capital of Richmond. Union troops met Confederate soldiers in a wilderness area in Spotsylvania County, Virginia. No one realized at first how serious it was. Then word reached Washington that more than 2700 men had been killed and 13,000 wounded.

The Sanitary and Christian Commissions were not prepared with enough supplies and volunteers. Suddenly Barton got her passes. Soon she was wading through red mud in the pouring rain along the banks of Acquia Creek near Fredericksburg.

Barton found at least 200 six-mule army wagons crowded with wounded men unable to move to safety because their wheels had sunk up to the hubs in mud. A young clergyman with the Christian Commission asked her: "Madam, do you think those wagons are filled with wounded men?"

Barton said she was sure they were.

"What can we do for them?" he asked.

"They are hungry and must be fed," she said.

The young man seemed unsure what to do next, so Barton took charge. She built a fire and made coffee. She showed him how to tie a tablecloth around his waist like an apron to carry the largest possible supply of crackers, while still leaving the hands free.

At last they headed toward the wagons of wounded. The young man stared at the mud. "How are we to get to them?"

"There is no way but to walk," answered Barton, and she led him into the mud that nearly reached their waists.

Barton discovered a much more serious problem in the city of Fredericksburg itself. Many of the soldiers' troubles, she believed, were caused not by the enemy but by improper behavior by "heartless, unfaithful officers" in charge of the city. "A dapper captain [staying] with the owners of one of the finest mansions in the town, boasted that he had changed his opinion since entering the city the day before; that it was in fact a pretty hard thing for refined people like the people of Fredericksburg to be compelled to open their homes and admit 'these dirty, lousy, common soldiers,' and that he was not going to compel it."

Barton walked through a crowded hotel, where more than 500 men lay helpless on the cold, bloody floor begging for water. Hundreds of army wagons lined the street, with no place to put the wounded.

Barton was furious. She found an army wagon to take her to the train 10 miles away. By train, she arrived in Washington at dusk. Immediately she went to see her close friend Henry Wilson, who was chairman of the Military Committee of the Senate. At 10 that night, he reported her story to the War Department, but they would not believe him. The officers in charge at Fredericksburg had reported no such suffering, they said. But Wilson had faith in Barton's story, and he offered them a choice: send out a party to investigate at once, or face the Senate tomorrow.

At two o'clock in the morning, a War Department committee left for Fredericksburg. They arrived at 10. By noon, the wounded men were being fed by the city, and the grand homes of Fredericksburg were opened to the soldiers. Many a man who might otherwise have died waiting for treatment lived to tell of Barton's tireless work during those difficult days.

Barton worked among the wounded at Fredericksburg for three more weeks. By June, Grant and Lee were in a standoff near Petersburg, Virginia. Grant swore he would fight on "if it takes all summer." Barton begged Wilson to help her join the troops at Petersburg. Wilson gave her a letter of introduction to General Benjamin F. Butler, in command of the Army of the James. He gave her a job as supervisor of diet and nursing at the army corps hospital near Point of Rocks, Virginia. Barton later claimed that she had served as Superintendent of the Department of Nurses for the Army of the James, but there is no official record of such a position.

Regardless of her position, she worked there for the rest of the war. She nursed a continuing flow of soldiers, including many of the U.S. Colored Regiments, made up of liberated or escaped slaves who had joined the fight.

It was here, in October 1864, that Barton saw her brother Stephen again. He had been captured on September 25 by the Union army, who had confiscated $1,000 from him and taken him to Norfolk, Virginia, as a prisoner of war. Barton used her influence with General Butler to have Stephen and all his papers brought to Port Royal. Things had been hard in North Carolina for Stephen, a Union sympathizer trying to stay on the good side of the Rebels. But Stephen had been violating the Federal blockade, which was meant to keep Northern goods out of the South during the war. He had been selling cotton to Northern factories in exchange for medical supplies badly needed by his Southern neighbors—and he had also earned substantial profits for himself.

Stephen had been badly treated in the Norfolk prison, and now he was ill. General Butler presided over Stephen's court-marital in November and ruled in his favor. Barton took care of Stephen during the winter. When he was transferred to a Washington hospital, Barton went with him. He died on March 10. His money was never returned.

During these months, General Grant had relentlessly attacked General Lee's army, encamped in the breastworks—deep trenches dug in the earth—around Petersburg. Finally, on April 2, 1865, Union forces broke through Confederate lines. Lee's small, tattered army fled south, and Jefferson Davis's Confederate government evacuated Richmond. On April 3, the Southern capital was in Union hands.

Six days later, on Palm Sunday, General Lee met General Grant at the McLean House in the small Virginia town of Appomattox Court House and surrendered. A few small battles would still take place. But for all practical purposes, the war was over.

Barton had devoted four long years of her life to reducing the suffering of the war. She and thousands of other women had played a substantial role. Women entered the war years unprepared for the horrors they would face, but they learned what to do by doing, and rose to the occasion with the courage of soldiers. Men had learned that women could do their part. But perhaps even more important, women learned themselves just how much they could do.

THE RAVAGES OF WAR

"Victory, yes! but oh, the cost!"

BARTON, *Reflecting on the
loss of life during the Civil War*

arton's work caring for the wounded on Civil War battlefields was over, but the wounds of the nation would take generations to heal. Five days after Lee surrendered at Appomattox, President Abraham Lincoln attended a play at Ford's Theatre in Washington and was assassinated by John Wilkes Booth. Overnight, the capital plunged from the heights of celebration to the depths of shocked mourning. Barton was heartsick.

Before Lincoln's death, Henry Wilson had helped her obtain the president's support for a new mission—the search for missing men. Every battle resulted not only in known dead and wounded, but also in a list of "missing." Some bodies were simply never found. Others were buried in unmarked graves. Thousands of men just disappeared. Some were deserters. Others perhaps took advantage of a chance to start a new life somewhere else.

The War Department had no system for tracing these lost men. Poor records were kept when prisoners of war were exchanged. The records from army hospitals were incomplete or did not exist. The families of missing men could do nothing but wait and hope.

During the war, Barton had filled her diaries with the names of wounded and killed soldiers. Now she proposed to become a clearinghouse for information. She would publish lists of missing men and invite the public to write her if they knew what had happened to them.

Barton went to Annapolis, Maryland, where she was given a tent, a few clerks, a small postage budget, and a title: "General Correspondent for the Friends of Paroled Prisoners." She sat down to bushels of mail, and received at least a hundred letters a day.

Barton's plan was to circulate lists of missing men through newspapers, post offices, and various organizations. By the end of May, she had her first list of missing men to publish. Most newspapers printed Barton's list free of charge, and hundreds of men wrote to give word of a friend they had fought with during the war. Most responses to Barton's work were full of praise. Sometimes, however, she found men who did not want to be found.

Madam:

I have seen my name on a sheet of paper somewhat to my mortification, for I would like to know what I have done, so that I am worthy to have my name *blazoned* all over the country. If my friends in New York *wish* to know where I am, let them wait *until* I see fit to write them. As you are anxious of my welfare, I would say that I am just from New Orleans, discharged, on my way North, but unluckily taken with *chills* and *fever* and could proceed no farther for some time at least. I shall remain here for a month.

Barton's response was in the scolding tones of a schoolteacher:

Sir:

I enclose copies of two letters in my possession. The writer of the first I suppose to be your sister. The lady for whose death the letter was draped in mourning I suppose to have been *your mother.* Can it be possible that you were aware of that fact when you wrote that letter? *Could* you have spoken thus, knowing all?

The cause of your name having been "blazoned all over the country" was your unnatural concealment from your nearest relatives, and the great distress it caused them....It seems to have been the misfortune of your family to think more of you than you did of them, and probably more than you deserve....I cannot apologize for the part I have taken. You are mistaken in supposing that I am "anxious for you welfare." I assure you I have no interest in it, but your accomplished sister, for whom I entertain the deepest respect and sympathy, I shall inform of your existence lest you should not "see fit" to do so yourself.

One day in June 1865, she received a letter from Dorence Atwater, a discharged soldier from Connecticut. He had been one of the first soldiers sent to the Confederate Andersonville Prison in Georgia. Because of his fine handwriting, he had been ordered by his captors to keep a list of all the prisoners who died. Conditions at most prisons were horrible during the war, but Andersonville Prison became infamous for its lack of food, rampant disease, and brutal treatment of prisoners. When the deaths passed 700 a week, Atwater had feared the Confederates might one day try to destroy or alter the records. So he began to keep a duplicate list, which he hid in the lining of his coat. When he was released at the end of the war, his list contained 14,000 names.

Atwater told Barton that the graves at Andersonville had been marked not by names but by numbered sticks, and his list included those numbers. When word reached Secretary of War Edwin Stanton, he sent a group—including Clara Barton and Dorence Atwater—to investigate the prison so that the graves could be properly marked. Eventually it was made into a national cemetery.

After their expedition to Andersonville, however, Atwater was arrested by the government and charged with stealing the list. They said it was government property now, because they had given Atwater $300 and a job as a clerk in exchange for the list. Atwater maintained that the list still belonged to him. He had only sold the government the right to *copy* the list. He feared that if the government kept it, the information might never reach the families

At Andersonville Prison in Georgia, Union soldiers lived in inhuman conditions.

of the dead soldiers. Barton used her influence to fight on Atwater's behalf, and eventually he was released from prison. Later, she worked with Atwater in getting his list published as a pamphlet.

By Christmas after the war's end, Barton was nearly out of money. She had lost her job at the patent office in August, leaving her no income at all. She was not successful raising money from private sources, and her efforts to have her work become part of the war department failed. She spent the holidays in a deep depression.

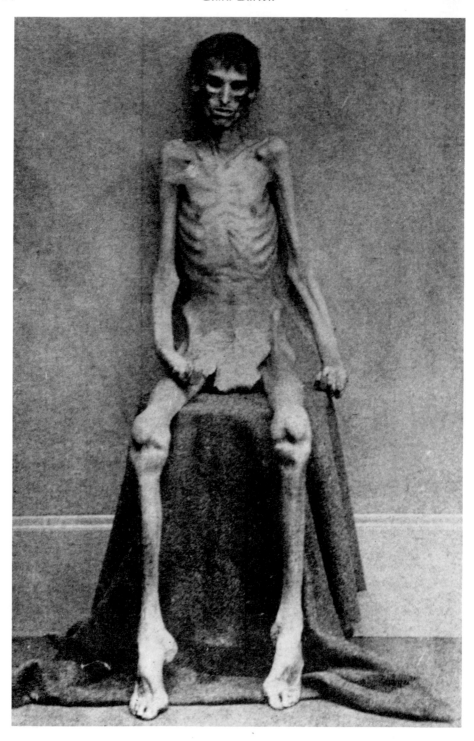

Pictures like this of prisoners at Andersonville shocked the people of the North.

In January 1866, however, Frances Gage came to visit her. She helped Barton write a petition to Congress that brought her $15,000 to continue her work.

Gage also urged Barton to travel the country and lecture on her war experiences. Barton had doubts about her ability to speak before large, curious crowds. She was fearless when devoting herself to others on the battlefield. But she had never fully outgrown her childhood shyness around strangers. "To this day," she wrote in *The Story of My Childhood,* "I would rather stand behind the lines of artillery at Antietam, or cross the pontoon bridge under fire at Fredericksburg, than to be expected to preside at a public meeting."

Barton tried it, however, and the public flocked to hear her speak. Dressed in black silk, she would stand before the audience as she once had before the classroom. She spoke in a clear, strong voice and filled her stories of the battlefield with dramatic details. She earned $75 to $100 a night and sometimes spoke as many as 14 times a month. The money helped finance her work tracing missing soldiers. It gave her financial independence. It also kept her name and her story before the public.

During this time, Barton developed a strong relationship with feminist leaders Elizabeth Cady Stanton and Susan B. Anthony, who were also on a lecture tour. They promoted her lectures, and she began to speak out for woman suffrage—the right of women to vote. Women had proved their worth in the war, she said. Her appeal to veterans of the war was bold: women were their faithful friends in the war. Now it was time to give women friendship and support in return.

Barton traveled and lectured for nearly two years. Her work tracing missing soldiers was nearly ended. Her office had answered 63,182 letters; 22,000 missing men had been identified. By the spring of 1868, she was worn out. Finally, Clara Barton lost her voice right in the middle of a lecture. Her old symptoms of nervous exhaustion returned. Doctors insisted that there was only one cure: go abroad for a few years and do absolutely nothing but rest.

Barton put her affairs in order and then packed her bags. She would go to Europe. But as for doing nothing but rest—that would prove to be one thing that Clara Barton found impossible.

A New War

"Now wasn't that the last thing you would have thought of, that I should come to Europe and set up *dressmaking,* and *French* dressmaking at that?"

BARTON, *On sewing workrooms she set up for the victims of war*

hile Barton was in Europe, she met a man named Dr. Louis Appia. He was a member of the International Convention of Geneva—also known as the Red Cross. He had an interesting story to tell her. In 1862, a young Swiss named Jean-Henri Dunant had published a book called *A Memory of Solferino.* In it he wrote about the suffering he had seen in 1859 during the Battle of Solferino. Dunant had proposed setting up an organization that would ready itself in peacetime for relief work in the time of war.

This was an exciting new idea, one that led to the Geneva Convention of 1864. Eighteen countries signed the Treaty of Geneva, which set guidelines for humane treatment of the wounded in wartime. An international organization was formed that operated independently of any country. It would take no sides in any war. The symbol chosen to signify its neutrality, or independence was a red cross on a white background. The symbol was like the Swiss flag, but with the colors reversed.

Dr. Appia knew of Barton's work during the Civil War. He asked her why the United States had refused to sign the Geneva

Treaty. Barton was surprised. She had never heard of the treaty. She assured him that the American people could not have heard of it either. Barton eagerly read the pamphlets he gave her. But she did not yet realize it would be a major part of her future.

Barton was still in poor health and could not shake her depression. Then on July 18, 1870, France declared war on Prussia. Barton awoke from her depression as if from a deep sleep and volunteered to work for the Red Cross.

Barton arrived in Basel, Switzerland, and was stunned by what she saw: the Red Cross was prepared with well-organized store-houses, filled with supplies from countries all over Europe. Armies of trained nurses stood ready to go to work. It far surpassed anything she had seen during the Civil War.

She said later in a lecture on the war: "I . . . saw the work of these Red Cross societies in the field, accomplishing in four months under this systematic organization what we failed to accomplish in

four years without it—no mistakes, no needless suffering, no starving, no lack of care, no waste, no confusion, but order, plenty, cleanliness, and comfort whenever that little flag made its way, a whole continent marshalled under the banner of the Red Cross—as I saw all this, and joined and worked in it, you would not wonder that I said to myself, 'If I live to return to my country, I will try to make my people understand the Red Cross and that treaty.'"

Barton spent most of the war providing aid to civilians. She had not witnessed the horrible suffering among Southern civilians during the American Civil War, so she was shocked by what she saw in Europe. Thousands were left homeless. The hospitals were filled with innocent victims, including hundreds of women and children. Yet Barton was not satisfied jut to ladle out soup to the crowds who came crying for food. The war had turned good people into beggars and vagrants. She saw what it did to their pride.

What people needed most next to food was clothing. The most common skill among the women was sewing. With the help of The Grand Duchess Louise, daughter of Kaiser Wilhelm of Germany, Barton organized a sewing workroom in Strasbourg. This gave the women of the city a chance to work and clothe their families. Soon they were even sending clothes throughout the region. Each worker received two francs per garment—and a new sense of self-respect. Later, Barton spent several months helping the homeless in Paris.

When she returned to the United States, Barton was surprised to find crowds waiting to welcome her home. She was even honored at a reception before returning to North Oxford.

Soon after, however, her sister Sally died of cancer. The death of her friend Henry Wilson added to her depression. She grew cross with friends. Though she had a comfortable savings, she began to fear she would become a burden. She lost all faith in doctors and medicine. Her friends and family did not know how to help her.

In 1876, a friend convinced her to go to a Dansville, New York, sanitarium, called "Our Home on the Hillside." What Barton found there was good food, good friends, and a belief that good health was possible. She learned how to take care of her health

This photo was taken before Barton founded the Red Cross. She later had the cross painted onto her brooch.

herself. She would never again suffer nervous breakdowns from stress. She was so taken with the town and its people that she bought a home and lived there for the next 10 years. Minna Kupfer, a young Swedish woman she had met in Europe, came to work as her housekeeper.

As her health returned, Barton began to look for work to fill her idle hands. Once again, she began to think of the International Red Cross and the Treaty of Geneva. One day she was visited by Julian Hubbell, a young chemistry teacher who had read of Barton's work during the Civil War. They talked of many things, including the Red Cross and the Treaty of Geneva.

Hubbell was fascinated. "What can I do?" he asked.

"Get a degree in medicine," she advised.

His regard for her was so great that he did just that—he quit his job and enrolled in the University of Michigan Medical School. They kept in touch while Barton began to work on a plan. It was a plan that would once again give her something meaningful to do— one that would put her whole life's work to good use.

Clara Barton was going to bring the Red Cross to the United States.

THE RED CROSS

"In time of peace and prosperity, prepare for war and calamity."

MOTTO OF THE INTERNATIONAL RED CROSS

In the spring of 1877, war broke out between Russia and Turkey. Searching for a way to take part, 55-year-old Clara Barton came up with the idea of starting an American branch of the Red Cross to aid the victims of the war. The International Red Cross, led by President Gustave Moynier, supported her as its official representative in Washington.

Unfortunately, in the years right after the Civil War, many Americans did not want to hear about war. Barton did not let their lack of interest stop her. She talked to people in Washington and found that many simply did not understand the treaty.

It was simple, Barton explained. The treaty held no hidden promises or alliances. Its only goal was to ease the suffering of those wounded in war. The signers agreed that during a war they would not fire on hospitals. All doctors, nurses, and others working in hospitals would be treated as *neutrals*—as if they took no side in the conflict. Hospitals would care for all wounded soldiers as individual human beings, no matter which uniform they wore. Any civilians who took the wounded into their homes would be protected, too. The Red Cross flag—a bold red cross on a white field—would be the international symbol of neutrality.

An American Red Cross could only be founded with the backing of the government. In January 1878, Barton met with President Rutherford B. Hayes, and he expressed interest in the treaty. He referred her to the State Department, but neither the secretary of state nor his assistant would even see her.

Discouraged, she returned to her home in Dansville. It was a beautiful, restful place, with fruit trees and stables. Barton planted a vegetable garden and adopted a black-and-white kitten she named Tommy. She also in a sense adopted a substitute "family. "Fanny Atwater, sister of Dorence Atwater, came to join Minna Kupfer in keeping house for her. The large 12-room house was often filled with neighbors and visiting friends, who were likely to hear Barton reading poetry aloud. Every visitor was told of the Red Cross.

That fall of 1878, Barton published a pamphlet called "The Red Cross of the Geneva Convention: What It Is." She knew that few would be drawn to the Red Cross by its wartime goals. So she went beyond the words of the Geneva Treaty.

The Red Cross in peacetime could help the victims of natural disasters. A chapter in every state would stand ready with food, clothing, and medical personnel. It would respond immediately in times of hurricane, earthquake, flood, or drought.

When James A. Garfield was elected president in 1880, Barton went to see him about the Red Cross. Garfield was interested. But not long after, he was assassinated.

Barton did not give up hope. She sought support from powerful organizations such as the Associated Press and a veterans' group called the Grand Army of the Republic, or the G.A.R. She won support from feminists such as Susan B. Anthony, who saw the Red Cross as a chance for women to hold positions of importance in a strong organization. In May 1881, Barton and supporters set up the first chapter of the American Association of the Red Cross in Dansville. Barton was elected president.

She was frustrated, however, by rival groups. One was the Women's National Relief Association, or the Blue Anchor. This group upset Barton the most, because it had been started by women who had once been her friends. They had grown resentful of what they saw as her domineering ways. The leaders of the Blue Anchor also wanted to become the American branch of the Red Cross. Barton worried endlessly that they might ruin her chances.

A natural disaster brought Barton's Red Cross chapter its first chance to prove itself. In the fall of 1881, forest fires raged across Michigan. Hundreds died, and thousands were left homeless. Barton contacted her young friend Julian Hubbell, who was still a medical student at the University of Michigan. He sent her reports of the damage and managed the local relief efforts. Rochester and Syracuse, other towns in New York State, set up Red Cross chapters and joined with Dansville to send money and supplies worth more than $80,000. Yet other, local relief agencies captured much of the publicity Barton had hoped to gain for the Red Cross.

Then in December of 1881, the new United States president, Chester A. Arthur, spoke in favor of the Treaty of Geneva in a speech to Congress. Barton moved back to Washington and worked harder to persuade senators and congressmen to vote for the treaty. She continued to seek the support of the press. At last, in March 1882, the Treaty of Geneva was unanimously ratified by the Senate and signed by President Arthur.

It was one of the greatest accomplishments of Clara Barton's life. Through her writing, lecturing, and lobbying, she had convinced the United States government to sign an international treaty of major humanitarian importance. She had helped move the United States from a young country turned inward on its own problems to one ready to take its place with the major nations of the world.

Soon, however, a new disaster demanded her attention. The Mississippi River flooded, destroying property and leaving hundreds of families homeless. Barton sent out a nationwide appeal for funds. Then she spent four months with Dr. Hubbell and a handful of workers distributing food, clothing, and medicine, and helping the families put order back into their lives.

Even after the Treaty of Geneva was signed, however, there were problems to be faced. The biggest one was money. Barton had used much of her own money in starting and running the Red Cross.

Now she felt the government should give the society an annual sum of money. Congress, however, refused to give it federal funds. If it gave money to the Red Cross, every other charitable group and society would be demanding money, too.

There was another problem. The government had approved the Treaty of Geneva, but it had not formally recognized Barton's organization as the official American branch of the International Red Cross. Among others, the Blue Anchor was still competing with Barton for official recognition. Barton's persistent work at last won her the government's approval. Then on June 9, 1882, the International Committee formally accepted Barton's Red Cross as its official American representative.

Barton had set up the Red Cross offices in a small ivy-covered row house at 947 T Street in Washington. The goal of the Red Cross would be to fill the gap between the disaster and the government's arrival. The Red Cross would not hand out money. In the first days of a disaster that destroyed businesses, farms, and homes, there was often nothing to spend money on anyway. Instead, the Red Cross would bring what people needed right away: food, clothing, blankets, and shelter.

Barton hoped to find someone to share the leadership of the Red Cross, but after a while she gave up looking. Her style of running the organization was her own, and it did not please everyone. She was used to having things done her own way. Workers sometimes felt she was looking over their shoulders. But no one could ever question her complete devotion to the organization.

In January 1883, she heard from her friend Benjamin Butler, with whom she had worked during the war. He was now governor of Massachusetts, and he asked her to take a job as female superintendent at the Massachusetts Reformatory Prison for Women, in Sherborn. It was entirely run by women committed to prison reform. Barton did not want to take the job, but Butler had never said no to her many requests during the war. In April 1883, she accepted—but only for six months.

Unlike many prisons, the Massachusetts Reformatory did not depend on physical punishment to control its inmates. The rooms were comfortable, the food was good, and women were allowed to bring their infants. Most of the women were young and poor. Barton saw that many of them were victims of a male-oriented society. They had been sentenced by all-male juries. Most were in prison for drunkenness or for "offenses against chastity"—crimes for which men could not even be tried.

Barton treated the women kindly—not as criminals—and they loved her. She set up boxes where they could write her with suggestions or complaints, and she answered every letter. The women worked daily sewing shirts or doing laundry. Barton thought they needed fresh air and sunshine, so she started a farm on the grounds so the women could sometimes work outside. In the wee hours of the morning, she kept up with her Red Cross work.

When Barton's work there was over, she took with her a stronger understanding of the double standard society forced upon women.

In February 1884, the Ohio River flooded. Barton immediately went to Pittsburgh, then Cincinnati, and she was shocked by the destruction she saw. The government brought aid, too, but mostly to the larger cities. Barton hired a boat named the *Josh V. Throop* and spent three months traveling up and down the river bringing relief to out-of-the-way places, to people who might otherwise be forgotten. With a handful of Red Cross workers, she handed out food, clothing, blankets, and coal.

Barton's work was completely sincere, yet she also saw the publicity value in sailing dramatically to shore with desperately needed goods. Reporters followed the boat, writing heartbreaking stores of the people she helped.

Barton earned a great deal of publicity for her work and the Red Cross with the story of "The Little Six," published in the Erie *Dispatch* on Monday, March 24, 1884.

Six children from Waterford, Pennsylvania, had put on a show and raised $51.25 for the victims of the Ohio flood. The children then sent the money to the *Dispatch* and asked the paper to send it where it would do the most good. The *Dispatch* sent it to Barton.

She was delighted with the children's gift and insisted on keeping it separate from other donations. She would save it until she found the best use for it—and the best opportunity for publicity. At last she found it at a place known as "Cave-in-Rock." A widow and her six children had lost their home in the flood. With a glance at Barton, Dr. Hubbell said, "Here are six children."

They gave the woman and her six children the money from the "Little Six," plus extra to make $100. Would that help?

The woman was speechless. Then she said she and her boys would build a new house, "and I shall name it 'The Little Six.'"

Stories like this provided the publicity Barton had long sought for her organization. Money poured in—and so did letters from people wanting to start their own local Red Cross chapters. In 1882, the Red Cross had raised $8,000. In 1884, the year of Barton's river trip on the *Josh V. Throop*, the society brought in $175,000.

In June, Barton returned to Washington. Mountains of Red Cross paperwork awaited her. It was too much for her. She went home to Dansville to rest, but she kept her condition a secret. There were those who thought she was too old to be doing work in the field—too old to be running the Red Cross. She became very sensitive about her age. She was in her sixties, though she looked and acted much younger. She dyed her hair and skillfully applied makeup to make herself look younger. She wore bright colors and even stuffed tissue paper into her bodice to give herself a more youthful-looking figure. Those who dared to baby her like an old lady received a sharp reply.

So when the secretary of state insisted she be the one to attend the Third International Conference of the Red Cross, she could not say no. It was quite an honor. Barton was the first woman ever appointed as a diplomatic representative by the United States government. When she arrived in Geneva, Switzerland, on September 1, 1884, only four other women were among the 85 delegates from 22 countries. Barton gave a speech on her work in the Civil War and her methods for identifying dead and wounded soldiers. She also told how she had used Red Cross services in peacetime to help the victims of natural disaster.

The international society was so impressed by her work that the members voted to amend the treaty to include peacetime relief work. In honor of Barton, they named it the American Amendment.

It was one of Barton's greatest contributions to the world. She had not just taken the idea of the International Red Cross and put it to work in the United States. She had expanded its vision. She had given it a new mission that would bring hope to millions of disaster victims around the world.

In May 1889, she led Red Cross efforts in Johnstown, Pennsylvania. Spring rains had flooded the town. Then a dam broke and a 30-foot wall of water crashed over the town. More than 2000 people died. Barton left for the area as soon as possible, and it took nearly five days to get through. The destruction was staggering. Sixty-seven-year-old Barton set up work in a small tent; it would be five months before her work was finished. Iowa and Illinois sent carloads of lumber, and the Red Cross built a 2-story, 30-room "Red Cross Hotel," designed by Dr. Hubbell, to house the homeless.

Barton had never been satisfied just with providing "things," though. On July 27, in the midst of the ruins, she opened the hotel with a formal "five o'clock tea," for she knew the people's spirits needed rebuilding as well. The response to the hotel was so great that several more were built.

Barton was one of the last to leave. An editorial in the Johnstown *Daily Tribune* said: "Hunt the dictionaries of all languages through and you will not find the signs to express our appreciation of her and her work. Try to describe the sunshine. Try to describe starlight. Words fail...."

Once Johnstown was back on its feet, these "hotels" were dismantled. Barton brought the lumber to a piece of land she had bought with her own money in Glen Echo, Maryland, not far from Washington. Here, in 1891, she built a house that would become the warehouse and headquarters for the Red Cross—and often home for Barton and her staff.

For the next 13 years, Barton ran the organization with an iron hand. Wherever the Red Cross went, Clara Barton went, too: from

Barton brought her Red Cross to Johnstown, Pennsylvania, to help victims of the 1889 flood.

tornadoes in Louisiana to tidal waves in South Carolina; from famines in Russia to the Spanish-American War.

The 1880s and 1890s were years of mixed emotions for Barton. She was always happiest when busy, and work with the Red Cross filled her days. She lectured as often as possible on women's rights, and was a speaker at the First International Woman's Suffrage

Conference in Washington, D.C., in 1888. She was saddened, however, by the death of many old friends, including Frances Gage. In March 1888, she was crushed by her brother David's death, which appeared to have been a suicide.

Just as upsetting were the continuing problems with the Red Cross. Some of the local societies were strong and almost independent organizations. Others had become more like social clubs, spending more time and money on dances and parties than on relief efforts. Even worse, many once-loyal members of the Red Cross had grown unhappy with the way Barton ran the organization. They thought a woman in her seventies was too old to manage it properly. Many thought she was a one-woman dictator. Other critics spread rumors that she was living extravagantly off Red Cross funds. She was especially criticized for failing to keep records of how Red Cross money was spent.

Barton, however, was used to doing things her own way. As in the Civil War, she spent much of her own money on her relief work. Often she did not bother to keep her own money and Red Cross money separate. During a disaster, she was too busy to worry about keeping records. She often kept them in shoe boxes or on odd scraps of paper here and there. It was a lifelong habit that had worked well enough when she was one woman bringing life to soldiers on the battlefield. It did not work so well in a professional organization that handled millions of dollars in donations.

As criticism grew, Barton became defensive. In 1898, she published the 700-page *The Red Cross in Peace and War,* which gave her view of the organization's work. Meanwhile, feuding within the Red Cross grew worse. Mabel Boardman led a group of members who opposed Barton. At the annual meeting in 1902, they tried to force Barton out. Barton, however, gathered her supporters and was named president for life.

In 1904, the Senate investigated her handling of Red Cross money. She was cleared of any intentional wrongdoing, but Barton had finally had enough. On May 14, 1904, she resigned as president of the American Red Cross. She was 82 years old.

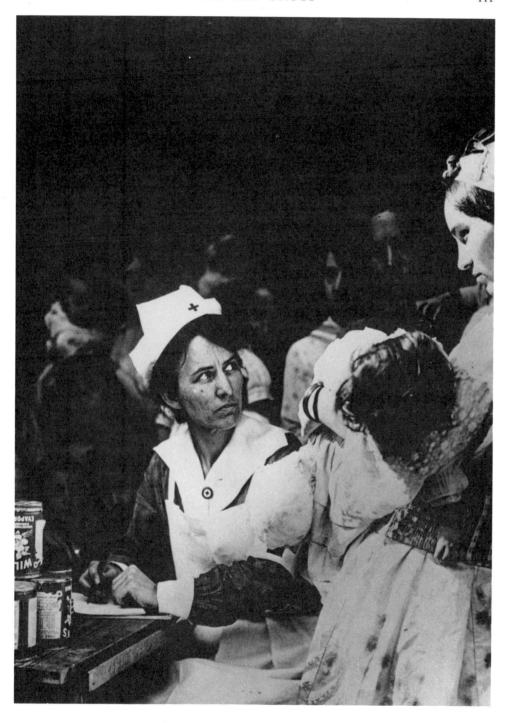

Red Cross workers aided victims and refugees in Europe during World War I.

It was a somewhat bitter end to her work in the Red Cross. She broke all ties with the association, now led by rival Mabel Boardman. Still, she believed she had given the world a great gift in creating the American Red Cross, and she hoped it would do well in the future.

Always the hard worker, Barton stayed busy during her last years. In 1905, she started the National First Aid Society. Where the Red Cross brought help in major disasters, the First Aid Society helped families with individual crises. In 1907, she published her small autobiography, *The Story of My Childhood*. Some years before, she had bought back one of the family farms in North Oxford. Now in her eighties, she still enjoyed working in the garden and taking long walks there or at the house in Glen Echo. She became interested in spiritualism and even astrology. Well into her eighties, she rose at dawn for a day full of chores and reading.

She grew lonely, however, as she lost many family members and friends.

At age 90, she suffered two attacks of double pneumonia. On April 10, 1912, she awoke from a nightmare. Dr. Hubbell was at her bedside, and she told him she had dreamed she was once again wading through blood on the battlefield: "I crept round once more, trying to give them at least a drink of water to cool their parched lips, and I heard them at last speak of mother and wives and sweethearts, but never a murmur or complaint. Then I woke to hear myself groan because I have a stupid pain in my back, that's all. Here on a good bed, with every attention. I am ashamed that I murmur." Then she slipped into unconsciousness.

On the morning of April 12, she awoke around nine o'clock, surrounded by Dr. Hubbell, a nephew, and her doctor.

"Let me go, let me go!" she cried.

With those words, she was gone.

Clara Barton was one of the great women of American history. She was not a saint, but a flesh–and–blood woman with strengths and weaknesses, convictions and insecurities. Yet it was her shortcomings as well as her special talents that made her the unique person that she was. She was born into an age when women married, had children, and "knew their place." Yet she carved out a new place for herself in life, supported herself, and prized her independence.

Her life was filled with contradictions: she was a woman who could hold her own in a man's world, but who was never quite happy in it either. Painfully timid and shy, she braved cannonfire and natural disasters to bring comfort to others. Her strong feelings of inadequacy and uselessness drove her to a life of usefulness and purpose. Her small pair of hands reached out to the hands of many, and she made a difference in thousands of lives.

The events of history brought Clara Barton a challenge that she met with energy, generosity, and spirit. On the battlefields of the Civil War, she fought against ignorance, sexism, and despair. She

Clara Barton fought ignorance and sexism to make nursing a respected and honorable profession.

helped change nursing from a menial chore to a respected profession. Her bravery and self-sacrifice helped earn new respect for the abilities of women.

In her work to create the American Red Cross, she was a persuasive politician, a master of public relations, and a tireless humanitarian. And she never questioned her right to take her place among men.

Often in her life she suffered from self-doubt. But her commitment as a feminist came from confidence in her right as a woman to take part in the world.

> Whenever I have been urged . . . to *ask* for this privilege for women, a kind of dazed, bewildered feeling has come over me. Of whom should I ask this privilege? Who possessed the right to confer [give] it? . . . Virtually there is no one to give her the right to govern herself, as men govern themselves, by self-made and self-approved laws of the land; but in one way or another sooner or later she is coming to it. And the number of thoughtful and rightful-minded men who will oppose, will be smaller than we think; and when it is really an accomplished fact, all will wonder, as I have done, what the question ever was.

But Clara Barton gave far more than her words to the women's movement. She gave her whole life. Unable to wait for the world to change, she dared to be a woman of intelligence and purpose—and she changed the world.

CLARA BARTON

December 25, 1821	Clarrissa Harlowe Barton is born in North Oxford, Massachusetts
1830	Is sent away to boarding school
1838	Becomes a teacher in North Oxford
1851	Barton's mother, Sarah, dies.
1852	Opens the first free public school in New Jersey
1860	Abraham Lincoln is elected president.
	South Carolina secedes from the Union.
1861	Confederates fire on Union troops at Fort Sumter—the Civil War begins.
	Barton helps nurse wounded soldiers in Washington, D.C.—her war service begins.
1862	Barton's father, Stephen, dies.
	Receives permission to nurse wounded soldiers on the battlefield
1864	Nurses wounded at Fredricksburg
1865	Begins work reuniting missing soldiers with their families
1869	Goes to Europe and learns of the International Convention of Geneva—the Red Cross
1870	Serves in the Internationl Red Cross in the Franco-Prussian War
1873	Returns to the United States and suffers a nervous breakdown
1881	Organizes the American National Red Cross and is elected the society's first president
1882	The U.S. Senate ratifies the Geneva Treaty.
1884	Serves as the United States' first female ambassador when she attends the first International Conference in Geneva
1898	Publishes *The Red Cross: A History*
1904	Resigns from the Red Cross
1907	Publishes *The Story of My Childhood*
April 12, 1912	Dies at her home in Glen Echo, New York, at the age of 90

Suggested Reading

*Bains, Rae. *Clara Barton, Angel of the Battlefield*. Mahwah, N.J.: Troll, 1982.

Barton, Clara. *The Story of My Childhood*. New York: Arno Press, 1980.

Boylston, Helen Dore. *Clara Barton, Founder of the American Red Cross*. New York: Random House, 1955.

*Hamilton, Leni. *Clara Barton*. New York: Chelsea House, 1987.

*Kent, Zachary. *The Story of Clara Barton*. Chicago: Childrens Press, 1987.

Klingel, Cynthia, and Dan Zadra. *Clara Barton*. Mankato, MN: Creative Education, 1987.

Ross, Mary Catherine. *Clara Barton, Soldier of Mercy*. New York: Grosset and Dunlap, 1960.

*Stevenson, Augusta. *Clara Barton, Founder of the American Red Cross*. New York: Macmillan, 1983.

*Readers of *Clara Barton: Healing the Wounds* will find these books particularly readable.

SELECTED SOURCES

CLARA BARTON

Barton, Clara. *The Red Cross in Peace and War*. Washington, D.C.: American Historical Press, 1899.

Barton, Clara. *The Red Cross of Geneva Convention: What It Is*. Washington, D.C.: R. H. Darby, 1878.

Barton, Clara. *The Story of My Childhood*. New York: Arno Press, 1980.

Barton, William E. *The Life of Clara Barton, Founder of the American Red Cross*. 2 vols. Boston & New York: Houghton Mifflin, 1922.

Epler, Percy Harold. *The Life of Clara Barton*. New York: Macmillan, 1915.

Pryor, Elizabeth Brown. *Clara Barton, Professional Angel*. Philadelphia: University of Pennsylvania Press, 1987.

THE CIVIL WAR

Catton, Bruce. *The American Heritage Picture History of the Civil War*. New York: American Heritage/Bonanza Books, 1960.

Catton, Bruce. *The Civil War*. New York: American Heritage Press, 1971.

Catton, Bruce. *Reflections on the Civil War*. New York: Berkley Books, 1982.

Davis, Burke. *The Civil War, Strange and Fascinating Facts*. New York: Fairfax Press, 1982.

McPherson, James M. *Battle Cry of Freedom*. New York: Random House, 1989.

The National Library of Medicine. *Medicine of the Civil War*. (undated pamphlet).

LETTERS

Frank Moore Papers, Manuscript Department, Duke University Library, Durham, North Carolina.

Mary Norton Papers, 1852-1895, Manuscript Department, Duke University Library, Durham, North Carolina.

INDEX

Cathy East Dubowski has written more than 25 books for children, including *Robert E. Lee and the Rise of the South* and *Andrew Johnson: Rebuilding the Union*, also in this series, and the Random House "Step into Reading" books *Pretty Good Magic* and *Cave Boy*. She currently works as a writer and editor in Chapel Hill, North Carolina, where she lives with her husband and five-year-old daughter, Lauren.